ADVANCE PRAISE

"Bill's memoir is a testament to the power of curiosity, perseverance, and passion for learning and innovation. I was fortunate to be his mentor at the Defense Mapping Agency, where I witnessed his breakthroughs in coding and cartography early in his career. He consistently impressed me with his drive, creativity, talent, approach to issues, and commitment to excellence. This book is an inspiring story of a dedicated public servant who made a real difference in the world."

—RICHARD A. BERG, PHD

"Bill's career exemplifies perseverance, dedication, and commitment to excellence. He rose through the ranks with a unique blend of technical expertise, leadership skills, and commitment to the mission. His memoir is an inspiring story of a public servant who made a real contribution to the mission and to the lives of countless individuals. Bill offers valuable lessons for anyone seeking to excel in their career. In my interactions with Bill, he was the hallmark of our Air Force Core Values: Integrity First, Service Before Self, and Excellence in All We Do."

—WILLIAM DONAHUE, LT. GEN, USAF (RETIRED)

"Bill James served on my staff during a time of immense technical change in our nation, politically and militarily. Laws requiring technical architectures, acquisition definitions, and even a role for a chief information officer were being promulgated. Bill used his intellect and, most importantly, his leadership skills to effectively deal with this dynamic environment and made lasting changes directly affecting mission accomplishment. This book is a must-read for those contemplating civil service and those currently serving who strive to be leaders."

—JOHN S. FAIRFIELD, LT. GEN, USAF (RETIRED), FORMERLY DEPUTY CHIEF OF STAFF, COMMUNICATIONS AND INFORMATION, PENTAGON

"Bill James provides his readers with a candid assessment of the triumphs and frustrations of government service from his unique perspective. I had the privilege of working alongside Bill in both the private sector and government and witnessed firsthand his leadership skills and ability to introduce cutting-edge processes to measurably improve government operations and missions, often in the face of stiff cultural opposition. Bill is one of those unsung heroes working behind the scenes, driving the adoption of technologies to improve the life outcomes of our Nation's citizens. This memoir chronicles Bill's inspiring journey of a man who found purpose and meaning in both the public and private sectors, while offering valuable insights and guidance to anyone contemplating a career in the complex yet rewarding world of government service."

—THE HONORABLE PAUL BRUBAKER, CHIEF MISSION OFFICER, DOMA TECHNOLOGIES, FORMER DEPUTY ASSISTANT SECRETARY OF DEFENSE, AND FORMER RESEARCH AND INNOVATIVE TECHNOLOGY ADMINISTRATOR AT US DEPARTMENT OF TRANSPORTATION

"Bill's dedication to serving Veterans was evident in every project he led at the VA. He was a tireless advocate for modernization and innovation, and he played a crucial role in transforming the agency's IT infrastructure to better serve those who have served our country. His memoir is a powerful reminder of the importance of leadership, collaboration, and commitment to excellence in public service."

—THE HONORABLE JAMES P. GFRERER,
CEO, FIDELIS TECHNOLOGY

THE ACCIDENTAL EXECUTIVE

THE ACCIDENTAL EXECUTIVE

FINDING PURPOSE IN PUBLIC SERVICE

FROM GS-1 TO THE SENIOR EXECUTIVE SERVICE

WILLIAM JAMES

COPYRIGHT © 2025 WILLIAM JAMES
All rights reserved.

THE ACCIDENTAL EXECUTIVE
*Finding Purpose in Public Service:
From GS-1 to the Senior Executive Service*

FIRST EDITION

ISBN   978-1-5445-4864-7 *Hardcover*
          978-1-5445-4863-0 *Paperback*
          978-1-5445-4865-4 *Ebook*

To my sons, Jason and Andrew. May you always find purpose and meaning in your lives.

CONTENTS

AUTHOR'S NOTE 13
INTRODUCTION 15

PART I: ROOTS TO ROUTINES
1. ROOTED IN HERITAGE 23
2. THE BOTTOM RUNG 31

PART II: POWER, PURPOSE, AND THE PATH AHEAD
3. FROM NIGHT SHIFTS TO NEW HORIZONS 43
4. FROM ELEVATION TO INNOVATION 61
5. LEADERSHIP IN THE MAKING 81

PART III: USTRANSCOM
6. DIGITAL HIGHWAYS 97
7. TRIAL BY FIRE 111

PART IV: SENIOR EXECUTIVE SERVICE
8. DIGITAL HIGHWAYS 127
9. THE LONG ROAD BACK TO PURPOSE 149
10. FROM LESSONS TO LEGACY 163
11. MISSION ACT 183
12. A FULL CIRCLE OF PURPOSE 203
13. CLIMBING THE LADDER 213

ABOUT THE AUTHOR 237

AUTHOR'S NOTE

Writing this memoir has been a journey of reflection, discovery, and gratitude. It's allowed me to revisit the pivotal moments, challenges, and triumphs that have shaped my life and career, and to share the lessons I've learned along the way.

This book is a testament to the power of public service and the profound impact it can have on individuals and communities. It's a story of resolve, resilience, and the enduring belief in the possibility of making a difference in the world.

I hope that by sharing my experiences, I can inspire others to pursue their own paths of service, to embrace challenges as opportunities for growth, and to never give up on their dreams.

I am deeply grateful to my family, friends, and colleagues who have supported me throughout my journey. Your encouragement, guidance, and friendship have been invaluable.

I also want to express my sincere appreciation to the men and women of the United States military and civil service. It has been an honor to serve alongside you and to witness your dedication, professionalism, and resolute commitment to our nation.

To write this book, I relied upon my civil service Official Personnel Folder, researched facts when I could, consulted with several of my colleagues, and called upon my own memory of these events and this time in my life. I chose to make this a "no names" memoir because I would not have been able to do service to the impact so many people had on my career. Many of the characters in this memoir are composite "mash-ups" of personalities of the people who influenced me. I occasionally omitted people and events, but only when that omission had no impact on the substance of the story.

Finally, to the readers of this book, thank you for joining me on this journey. I hope that my story will resonate with you and that you will find inspiration and encouragement within these pages.

INTRODUCTION

Imagine this: It's the summer of 1974, and as a young man, I faced a choice. Spend another hot and humid summer mowing lawns and lifeguarding under the blazing sun, or try something different? I opted for different and found myself sitting in a small office at Scott Air Force Base, starting my first civil service job as a lowly GS-1 clerk. My task? Filing contract change pages into three-ring binders. Mundane, monotonous, and utterly unremarkable—a temporary summer job—or so I thought.

Little did I know that this would be the first step on a journey that would take me from the depths of bureaucratic obscurity to the polished halls of power in the Pentagon, from filing papers to briefing generals on military policy. Along the way, I'd pioneer digital mapping technologies at the Defense Mapping Agency, wrestle with critical information technology failures at the US Transportation Command during Operation Desert Shield/Desert Storm, and ultimately help implement sweeping national healthcare reforms for Veterans at the Department of Veterans Affairs.

Early in my career, I spelled "veteran" with a lowercase "v." It wasn't until after joining the Department of Veterans Affairs as an SES that I truly came to understand, appreciate, and humbly respect the sacrifices America's military members make to protect our liberties. Since then, I always spell "Veteran" with a capital "V." You'll see this change in style reflected in accordance with that timeline in my memoir. It is not a typo.

This is a story about starting at the bottom and earning a seat at the top. It isn't just about climbing the career ladder within the government; it's about navigating the complex world of public service, including nearly two decades in the private sector supporting government IT initiatives. It's about embracing challenges, persevering through setbacks, and discovering the transformative power of service. It's about how a career in government, often misunderstood and undervalued, can lead to a life of meaning, impact, and extraordinary achievement.

This book goes beyond a personal journey to stand as a validation of the power of purpose. The message serves as a reminder that, regardless of where you are in your career or the challenges you encounter, fulfillment and the ability to make a meaningful impact can be achieved by committing yourself to a cause greater than your own.

In these pages, I invite you to walk alongside me as I navigate the twists and turns of a life in public service. I'll share the lessons I've learned, the challenges I've overcome, and the insights I've gained about leadership, resilience, and the true meaning of service. My hope is that by the end of this journey, you'll be inspired to find your own purpose, embrace your challenges, and discover the extraordinary impact you can have on the world.

To help you follow my journey, I've included simple timeline graphics at the beginning of each chapter that look like this.

When	1970	1972	1974	1976	1978	1980	1982	1984
Rank	GS-#			GS-#			GS-#	
Location	Organization/City							

These timelines will show my progression through the ranks of civil service, providing context for each chapter's experiences and challenges.

Early on, I didn't know where this path would take me. Returning to college after that first taste of government work, I felt the seed of public service begin to take root. By 1976, when an offer from the Defense Mapping Agency landed in my hands, the idea had developed enough to demand my full attention. No longer just a sprout of potential, the concept had grown into a flourishing opportunity, requiring a pivotal decision—whether to nurture this vision into a purposeful life or to set the path aside and pursue a different direction.

I felt the calling to contribute to something larger than myself, to be part of a mission that served the greater good, but choosing to pursue a career in civil service raised eyebrows. Many of my friends were chasing lucrative opportunities in banking and consulting, and some in my family saw a government job as a betrayal of their expectations. Their belief in the "lazy government employee" stereotype made it clear that, in their eyes, I'd chosen the path of least resistance. Why would I choose such an uninspired path, one burdened with assumptions of mediocrity, over the prestige and financial rewards of the private sector? Even I wrestled with those doubts.

But one piece of advice rang louder than their criticism. My grandmother, a strong woman of resilience and insight, once told me, "You're like a train on a track. Stay the course, and you'll reach your destination." Her words became more than just advice. They were a guiding principle. That saying reminded me that the path I was on, though challenging, would lead to something meaningful, provided I stayed steadfast and committed to my purpose.

Choosing purpose over prestige was not always simple or easy. Public service offered the chance to contribute to something bigger than myself, to be part of work that mattered. That realization became the foundation of my career and a source of quiet determination to find and prove, both to myself and to my skeptics, that a life in government service could be impactful and fulfilling.

Over the years, I came to fully appreciate the implicit "bargain" that civil servants accept and understand. Relatively low pay, job security, and a reliable retirement—the hallmarks of that bargain—were constants in my upbringing. But as a kid, I didn't know or understand the price that came with it. Only later did I realize the personal ambitions, job flexibility, and potential financial rewards my father had sacrificed, and eventually, I would make similar trade-offs in my own career. What I came to value was what I gained in return—a deep sense of fulfillment from working on projects with significant public impact. Whether supporting national defense or improving Veterans' access to healthcare, I found meaning in my work that far outweighed a paycheck or title.

My career, though ultimately rewarding, wasn't without its unexpected trials. Before it even officially began, I encountered something both shocking and deeply unsettling: sexual harassment during a job interview, an experience seldom discussed from my perspective of a straight white male. The experience left me reeling, my naive assumptions about the professional world shattered. But this encounter also ignited my resolve to build workplaces where professionalism wasn't limited to policy posters on a break room wall, but about cultivating a culture of mutual respect.

I led through a range of challenges big and small, from resolving critical IT failures during Operation Desert Shield/

Desert Storm to implementing the VA MISSION Act to improve Veterans' access to healthcare. Time and again, I found myself at the intersection of chaos and opportunity, solving problems and driving innovation in systems that weren't designed for speed or flexibility. Along the way, I collected a trove of "inside baseball" stories—moments of triumph, frustration, and everything in between—that carried lessons about leadership, persistence, and the art of navigating the most rigid systems.

Civil service is unglamorous, frustrating, complex, and often misunderstood. But it is also immensely rewarding. By following my unlikely path from a GS-1 clerk to a member of the Senior Executive Service (SES), I hope readers will see that meaningful success is attainable, even in the most complex and frustrating environments. Above all, my story is a reminder that purpose and impact are worth pursuing, no matter where your career path takes you.

And for those aspiring to attain the rank of Senior Executive Service, this memoir includes a guide, not a shortcut, built from my own experiences. In Chapter 13 (Supplement), I've distilled my journey into fifteen steps that guided me on the path to that highest level of career government service. These steps, born from experience and refined through reflection, are proof of the power of perseverance, strategic thinking, and a commitment to excellence.

Come walk with me through the halls of government and the corridors of industry. Discover the lessons I learned, the missions I embraced, and the pursuit of purpose that defined my career. Whether you're an experienced civil servant, just starting your career, or considering your calling, I hope this story will inspire you to find value in your work and remind you of the quiet satisfaction that comes with making a difference. Turn the page and discover the lessons I learned along the way.

PART I

ROOTS TO ROUTINES

FINDING MYSELF AS A GS-1

Part I captures my journey from a small-town dreamer to someone stepping into the complexities of the wider world. It begins with the curiosity of childhood and leads to a defining moment—starting as a GS-1 clerk at the Defense Communications Agency (DCA). Meant to be just a summer job, an alternative to lifeguarding and mowing lawns, it became so much more than that. It was more than a job; it was a turning point.

Starting at the very bottom of the federal ladder was humbling, but it shaped me in ways I couldn't have imagined. My first supervisor, with her kindness and patience, taught me how to navigate the intricacies of government work while showing me the value of service and strong people skills. Those early days left me with a deep appreciation for the significance of even small roles and the potential for development they offer.

This part of my story is more than a recounting of milestones. It's a reflection on how the beginning of something, no matter how modest, can spark profound growth and set the stage for a lifetime of purpose and service. It celebrates those humbling early days, the importance of showing up, and the realization that the lessons we learn in service to others often shape the person we become.

CHAPTER 1

ROOTED IN HERITAGE

AIMING FOR THE HORIZON

"If a part doesn't fit, turn it upside down and try it again."

—MAX JAMES

This simple advice from my father, shared countless times during my childhood, became a guiding principle throughout my life and career. It taught me the importance of adaptability, resilience, and approaching challenges from different perspectives.

When	1960	1962	1964	1966	1968	1970	1972	1974
Rank	Early Childhood and Teens						College	
Location	Lebanon, Illinois							

This timeline shows my early years, from childhood to college in 1974. These timelines will track the chapters of my career advancement, highlighting key milestones and providing a visual reminder of where I was at various stages of my journey.

MORE THAN A DOT ON THE MAP

Nestled amid the expansive flat farmland of Southern Illinois, the small town of Lebanon was my entire world during my formative years. To the unfamiliar eye, this quiet farming town might have seemed like one of many unremarkable dots on the map. But for me, it was a place rich in character, defined by its tightly knit community.

Lebanon sported a "main drag" lined with tiny shops tucked into Victorian buildings facing a wide brick main street that had once contained railway tracks leading west across the Mississippi River to St. Louis, a mere twenty miles away. Past downtown and just beyond the fields, Scott Air Force Base stood as a beacon, its low-slung buildings and long runways a constant reminder of the power and the might of our military. The base was a dynamic presence, contrasting with the surrounding farmland and tethering our town to a wider world. From time to time, we'd hear the distant rumble of a jet taking off or even experience the thrilling jolt of a sonic boom that rattled our windows. The silvery contrails that streaked across the sky became a familiar symbol of ambition and human ingenuity. From the moment I entered kindergarten until graduating with a degree in mathematics from Lebanon's McKendree College, my world remained confined to the familiar boundaries of that sleepy little town.

Lebanon was a vibrant community rich in history, with quaint buildings and farm fields. It was a racially diverse community, filled with friendly faces and shared values. Growing up there meant getting to know your neighbors and relying on each other. For a kid like me, it also meant having the freedom to explore. I spent countless hours wandering through the fields and wooded areas around town, discovering hidden corners, observing wildlife, and unraveling the secrets of nature. Scouting enriched these ventures further, instilling in me a sense of curiosity and teaching me the importance of leadership, teamwork, and self-reliance—values that would guide me throughout my life. There was no shortage of lessons to be learned.

From the age of five until I graduated from college, I shared endless hours with my father, fixing things—houses, cars… anything that needed to be repaired. Over the years, I learned plumbing, wiring, and how to tinker with engines. My father had grown up in a small town in western Illinois, where he learned what all farmers learned: independence, how to complain about the weather, and how to fix anything, because crops and livestock won't wait for a repairman to show up. These were essential skills that formed the foundation of my problem-solving abilities.

MORE THAN I KNEW

My father was a World War II veteran. A month before his eighteenth birthday, he had enlisted in the US Navy and served in the war's Pacific Theater as a "sparky," an Electrician's Mate aboard ships. He received his basic naval training a thousand miles from the nearest ocean at the US Naval Training Station on the Great Lakes in North Chicago. Dad became a journeyman electrician and gained experience installing and repairing electrical systems and telephone circuits in the bowels of ships.

Growing up, that's all I knew about my father's service. Later, I discovered he had taken radar training. Radar was brand new in 1944. Although primitive by today's standards, World War II Navy radar was used not only to detect enemy aircraft but also to track various types of weather, including the devastating Typhoon Cobra that struck the US Pacific Fleet near the Philippines, where my father was stationed at the time.

In the Navy, my father built his problem-solving abilities and enjoyed hands-on learning. He also discovered he was good at math. Not only was he good at it, but he loved it. After being honorably discharged in 1946, he returned home to his parents' farm and continued his education by taking additional coursework in general engineering and mathematics. Later, he put his radar training to work, accepting a position in government civil service where he managed maintenance programs for weather radar systems for the US Air Force Weather Service at Scott Air Force Base in Southern Illinois.

TURNING THINGS UPSIDE DOWN

My father believed he could fix anything, and at his knee, I learned the home handyman and car mechanic skills needed to put virtually anything back together. At night, after supper at our kitchen table, he and I would spend hours doing math problems. One math problem we loved to work on together was solving quadratic equations by completing the square. That was my favorite problem, because the answer was *hidden* inside the equation. All I had to do was manipulate the numbers and variables to force the answer to reveal itself.

Now, that may sound quirky, but my dad was a quirky and loving man who wore bow ties long after they'd gone out of style. And among the usual Christmas gifts of toys and clothes, there was always some special gadget waiting for me under the tree, chosen with a sparkle of anticipation in his eyes. Those moments of play and humor taught me that curiosity wasn't limited to solving equations or fixing a pipe. The concept expanded to discovering joy in small things and embracing life with an open mind.

BATTLING GREMLINS

A hobby we shared was collecting and working on vintage cars. One memorable lesson he taught me while working on an old Studebaker was, "If a part doesn't fit, turn it upside down and try it again." That rarely worked, but the lesson wasn't in the action—rather, in the mindset. His point was, sometimes it is necessary to move a part or move yourself to gain a different perspective on the task at hand. He was teaching me to shift my approach when things didn't go as planned. This ability to rethink and tackle challenges from a fresh angle shaped not only the way I solved problems but also the way I approached life.

My father often joked that every inanimate object was home to mischievous gremlins, whose sole mission was to annoy us in any way possible. If an engine bolt fell out of my hands and landed in a clearly visible but very hot and inaccessible location, it was those darn little tricksters at work. When a tool broke, it was just the gremlins having fun. By blaming these annoyances on our invisible foes, he taught me to see setbacks as chances for perspective, not frustration.

My father also taught me that these gremlins can always be defeated with patience and perseverance. Just keep trying, and sooner or later, they'll give up. Looking back, I see that this mindset not only helped me handle daily challenges but also fostered a measure of emotional intelligence. By laughing at mishaps and persevering, I developed a healthier outlook on life's ups and downs and a more positive approach to new challenges.

As a by-product of this on-the-job training, or "OJT" handyman training, I embraced "learning through my fingers." That became my go-to method for grasping new concepts. More than just a phrase, the idea served as a philosophy that shaped my approach to learning and solving problems. For me, this meant embracing hands-on experiences, where a process of creating, building, or fixing something was about actively engaging with the process and understanding the underlying principles and mechanics. Whether I was hammering nails into wood, writing equations on paper with a pencil, or tightening bolts with a wrench, those tangible interactions helped me internalize concepts in a way that explanations never could. Those early lessons, the willingness to try to fix anything, intentionally changing perspectives, and my curiosity about how things work, have had a lasting impact on my life and career. These values were imparted as a way of fixing things and as a way of approaching many challenges in other areas of life.

FROM SMALL-TOWN ROOTS TO LIFE-ALTERING DECISIONS

A combination of farmers' self-reliance with the Air Force's core values of integrity, service, and excellence defined the culture of my small town. Despite the Leave-It-to-Beaver life I led, I was acutely aware of the larger world that existed beyond its borders. As I grew older, I thought about becoming an Air Force pilot, though I was aware my eyesight might be a hurdle. If that path wasn't possible, I saw joining the civil service, like my father, as a viable way to give back for the freedoms and the opportunities I enjoyed. With a government career, I believed I could make a positive impact using the values and lessons from my upbringing in this small town.

As I approached my senior year in high school, I stood in my bedroom and gazed out on the quiet streets of Lebanon. Due to my good ACT and other standardized test scores, and thanks primarily to my math results on those tests, I received acceptance letters from several colleges and universities. All of them, except for my hometown college, McKendree, required me to venture far beyond my comfort zone. Despite the allure of those new horizons, I found myself drawn back to the cozy familiarity of Lebanon. The thought of matriculating at a local institution; living at home to save some money, where I could walk to class if necessary; and knowing many of my classmates by name held a special charm.

And so, with a mix of excitement and trepidation, I made the decision that would shape the next few years of my life. I attended McKendree College, not because of its reputation or rich history as one of Illinois's oldest colleges, although these were certainly attractive features, but because I was searching for comfort, convenience, and being close to home. In October 1972, I matriculated at McKendree, declaring my major as mathematics and setting out on a journey that would be marked by familiarity, and later, a sense of stagnation. As I entered my sophomore year, I felt a hunger for something more.

I remember having a conversation with my father at Christmas about ideas for a summer job. He thought about the question and offered two intriguing options. One possibility was to assist his brother, my uncle, in his veterinary practice in Sullivan, Illinois, a two-hours' drive away. The other option was applying for a summer intern position at Scott Air Force Base. Both options appealed to me since they offered a chance to break free from the usual drill of lawn mowing and lifeguarding summer jobs. I could experience something truly different. And so, in February 1974, I made my way to the civilian personnel office at Scott Air Force Base, where I filled out an application with nervousness and anticipation. Little did I know that this decision would set in motion a chain of events that would change the course of my life forever. A couple months later, I received a letter—an official-looking document from the Defense Communications Agency announcing that my application had been accepted. I was to report for duty at the Defense Commercial Communications office at Scott Air Force Base in late June 1974. And with that, the curtain rose on the next act of my life's story, a journey marked by challenge, growth, and ultimately, transformation.

CHAPTER 2

THE BOTTOM RUNG

A GS-1 CLERK IN THE GOVERNMENT MACHINE

"The bureaucracy is expanding to meet the needs of the expanding bureaucracy."

—OSCAR WILDE

My first experience as a GS-1 clerk opened my eyes to the realities of government work, with its intricate processes, hierarchical structures, and sometimes mind-numbing monotony. But it also sparked a curiosity about the inner workings of this complex system and the potential for finding purpose within it.

When	Summer of 1974
Rank	GS-1
Location	Scott Air Force Base, Illinois

WHERE MISSION MET BUREAUCRACY

Scott Air Force Base bustled with activity. The site was a hub for Air Force medical evacuation missions, with planes taking off and landing, transporting military patients destined for hospitals at Scott Air Force Base and other medical treatment facilities in the United States. That would change over the years, as the base no longer supported those aeromedical missions, but back then, C-9 "Nightingale" hospital aircraft were a common sight on the very busy base, a place that echoed with the sounds of aircraft engines and the hustle of military personnel.

Scott AFB was well maintained, with neatly trimmed lawns and orderly World War II buildings reflecting the discipline and precision of the military, and the Air Force pride in, and compliance with, military appearance standards. At the edge of the base stood a low, nondescript office building. The year was 1974, and the world outside the windows was abuzz with change and upheaval in the Cold War, post–Vietnam War era.

The sign above the door read DEFENSE COMMUNICATIONS AGENCY. A white sign with black lettering next to the door read DEFENSE COMMERCIAL COMMUNICATIONS OFFICE, or DECCO. Crossing the threshold of this drab building, I stepped out of the steam of the Southern Illinois summer and into the soup of US government civil service, where mission met bureaucracy. Walking through the door and down the hall, plodding across the waxed and worn linoleum tile floor, I noticed a faint squeaking noise coming from my recently shined shoes. When I finally found the correct office number, I took a deep breath, squared my shoulders, and stepped into this strange new world, ready to face the challenges that lay ahead. The squeaking sound of my shoes stopped, replaced by a whisper of uncertainty.

THE TARIFFS LIBRARY

Entering the room, I was struck by the brilliance of fluorescent lights mixed with sunlight fighting its way through dirty windows. Tiny dust particles tumbled through the light in their slow descent onto faded green metal desks. The government-issued desks, though sturdy, showed signs of wear, their once-glossy surfaces marred by scratches, dents, and faded patches. An unmistakable air of shabbiness and muted efficiency hung in the room. The entire space was arranged in a utilitarian library-like layout, with the desks forming neat lines across the floor.

Each desk was cluttered with paperwork: manila folders and stacks of documents held together with black binder clips and rubber bands. The walls were a dull, institutional green adorned with typewritten announcements, policies, rules, and regulations. The slow-moving air held the scent of paper, ink, and stale coffee. Despite the drab atmosphere, a sense of purpose permeated the room as clerks and Air Force military personnel shuffled in and out, from desk to desk, each task contributing to the larger bureaucratic machine. Muffled conversations and the occasional rhythmic clatter of typewriters filled the air, punctuated by the occasional ringing of a rotary dial telephone, connecting personnel with colleagues and superiors across the country and across the world. These vintage devices, placed strategically on each desk, served as physical reminders of the office's primary mission.

At the far end of the room, a door opened to a vast library with row upon row upon row of gray metal library shelves lined with hundreds of black three-ring binders, each labeled meticulously, their spines bearing signs of frequent handling.

At the desk to my immediate right, a plump woman hunched over a typewriter. Her fingers danced on the keys as she typed up the latest status report for her boss. The clack-clack, rat-atat-tat of the machine formed a constant rhythmic soundtrack in the room. She noticed me, looked up, and smiled.

"Welcome," she said. "I assume you're Bill James, the new clerk. I'm glad to see you. Let me show you around."

The woman behind the typewriter was my first government supervisor. From her, I learned lessons about my performance in my job as a GS-1 tariffs clerk and set my expectations about the civil service system with its own rules, culture, and demands. So began my career as a GS-1 Clerk in the Tariffs Library of DECCO.

A ROOKIE'S SUMMER AS A TARIFFS CLERK

The GS in GS-1 stands for "General Schedule," a pay system used by the federal government to determine the salary of its employees. GS-1 clerks—positioned at the lowest rung of the government civil service ladder—were paid a low salary back then. My pay was two dollars and fifty cents an hour. Although the work was simple and menial labor, those three summer months ultimately were counted as official time toward my civil service retirement pension, a long-term benefit that stretched far beyond my immediate time horizon. My job was to help manage the DOD (Department of Defense) contracts for telephone circuits supporting the Automatic Voice Network, known simply as AUTOVON.

This telephone network was developed in the 1950s by AT&T for the US military and government agencies. During the Cold War, AUTOVON was an automated voice switching system that connected calls between different locations. As a tariffs clerk, I was responsible for receiving, accounting, and logging long-distance telephone company circuit records received from the only telephone company at the time, AT&T.

Whenever the DOD telecommunications lines were added or removed from service, or the contract for a line changed its price or terms, I was given a piece of paper that documented the contract change for the telephone circuit. My job was to find the three-ring binder in the tariffs library that held the old page and replace it with the new page. This search-and-replace task was simple but labor intensive, given the huge number of tariffs and the commensurate size of the tariffs library itself.

LEARNING THE ROPES

As I sat at my desk trying to wrap my head around this complex web of contracts, tariffs, and infrastructure, I couldn't help but feel a sense of wonder at the people who had designed and maintained this telecommunication system over the years. Such an enormous undertaking required precision, coordination, and a deep understanding of the requirements, the threats, and the complexities involved. The more I learned, the more I realized just how vital AUTOVON, and by extension, my role in keeping it up to date, were in keeping our country safe and connected.

As part of a government agency, I needed to learn the ropes. My supervisor, the woman who had halted her furious typing to welcome me to her team, took me under her wing and showed me the ins and outs of my new role. She explained the procedure for handling telephone calls, updating records, and communicating with other departments. As we walked through the office, she pointed out key personnel, introduced me to colleagues, and offered words of encouragement. I was struck by her patience, kindness, and willingness to answer all my questions, no matter how trivial or stupid they seemed. She took a genuine interest in helping me learn and adapt to the agency's unique culture. And there was always more to learn. In terms of my own performance, I would never achieve her level of expertise. Watching her work, I marveled at her ease in managing this complex system, effortlessly handling multiple tasks and responsibilities. As the days turned into weeks, I felt more comfortable in my new role. Through on-the-job training from this gentle woman, I learned the ropes and developed the skills I needed to succeed. Her mentorship and guidance were invaluable. I felt grateful for her willingness to take the time to teach me. In many ways, this training was also a crash course on bureaucratic protocol. I learned how to navigate the agency's complex systems, communicate effectively with colleagues, and prioritize tasks. Looking back, I realized the OJT she provided was a critical part of my learning experience. She not only taught me the technical skills I needed to perform in that simple role, but she also helped me understand the soft skills and knowledge required to survive and thrive in the complex, controlled civil service environment.

WHEN BRAVADO MEETS BUTTERMILK

I had my first real job, and things were off to a great start. A couple of weeks in, I was eager for some company to bolster my confidence. Walking into the cafeteria, I scanned the room for a potential conversation partner and spotted a cute tariffs clerk. I'd noticed her earlier that day in an office down the hall from mine. I took a deep breath to calm my nerves and approached her with a smile.

"You want to grab some lunch together?" I asked. She smiled back, and we walked over to the serving line together. As we waited in line, I asked her about herself. I was playing it cool and trying to sound suave, while really just wanting to make a good impression. Walking down the food line, determined to impress this young woman with my sophistication, I selected a small carton of buttermilk to go with my meal. Now, I had never drank buttermilk before, but I assumed it would be sweet, buttery, and rich. We found an empty table, and I carefully opened the carton of buttermilk, a confident smile spreading across my face.

My cute lunch partner raised her eyebrows and, with a look both curious and amused, said, "Do you like buttermilk?"

"Well, yes, I do," I said proudly. Surely, I was making an impression with my chosen drink. It was different. It was classy. Drinking buttermilk would make me unforgettable. I imagined more lunch dates in my future. With one deep breath, I took a huge gulp, while my charming lunch companion looked on expectantly.

The instant the sour-tasting liquid hit my tongue, disaster struck. My face twisted, I gagged, and despite my efforts to regain composure, it was too late. The damage was done. My lunch mate burst out laughing and I knew I'd been busted.

She said, "You know, Bill, you look like you just sucked on a lemon."

My face was on fire, red with embarrassment, but I laughed along with her. Clearly, as mortified as I was, she seemed to find my predicament amusing, possibly even endearing. From that point on, having exposed my stupid bravado and vulnerability, my cute coworker was friendly toward me. She answered my questions and taught me how things worked in the office. Perhaps the most important lesson was the one I taught myself with that buttermilk. To succeed, I had to be humble and open to connecting with others, even if it meant being vulnerable or making mistakes. The shared experience created a sense of camaraderie between us, and as a result, she was more willing to help me out and share her expertise at work.

Another, more serious lesson I discovered in this tiny rote summer clerical job was the magnitude of the DOD mission. I was like an ant tasked with a job of tracking the changes in hairs on an elephant. Finding the hairs was simplistic, monotonous work, but an appreciation of the size and the power of the elephant was beyond my comprehension. I began to know how much I didn't know.

CHOOSING A PATH BEYOND "GOOD ENOUGH"

In that summer of '74, as my GS-1 job came to an end, I headed back to my hometown college to finish my degree in mathematics. Walking out the door of the dusty old DECCO office building, I reflected on the lessons I'd gathered over the past three months: the necessity of humility; the significance of patience, kindness, and mentorship; and the invaluable experience gained from on-the-job training.

Although I enjoyed those three months as a civil servant, I wondered if the lifestyle afforded by a career in government civil service would be enough. The tension between mission-driven initiatives and the regimented world of bureaucracy was palpable. I had touched the bones of its organizational structure. Like a small gear escaping from an enormous clock, I was one small part of a great machine. I had contributed in a very small way to keeping its time and coordinating its movements. But was this what I wanted? After all, my father fed, clothed, and sheltered our family by accepting the government civil service "bargain" of a lifetime of relatively low pay in exchange for job security and, someday, a good pension. He'd worked tirelessly for decades, often at the expense of his own personal goals and aspirations, for the sake of providing stability and security for our family. A career in government was good enough for my father, and he provided our family with a good life.

My father never said this to me, but I'm sure he hated the saying "It's good enough for government work," a common idiom that implied a sense of mediocrity. The phrase suggested personal performance that is perhaps satisfactory but not impressive, innovative, or exceptional. To me, it was a derogatory phrase that implied a baseline of poor performance, which was acceptable to government workers but no one else. As I weighed my options, I wondered if I could find fulfillment in a career that was even associated with that phrase..."good enough for government work." As I pondered my career choices, I couldn't help but wonder if I could be happy in government service. The thought of being a minor cog in a vast machine, working diligently behind the scenes to benefit others without much recognition or reward, was both humbling and intimidating. Was it possible for me to find purpose and satisfaction in a career that didn't scream excitement or prestige? Could I be content with hoping that my work was making a difference, even if it wasn't always visible or acknowledged?

I took a deep breath, weighing my options. Could I find fulfillment in a career that prioritized stability, security, and service over recognition or financial gain? Was being "good enough for government work" going to be good enough for me?

PART II

POWER, PURPOSE, AND THE PATH AHEAD

Part II dives into a time of upheaval and growth, where unemployment loomed, and ambition simmered. I remember the weight of obligation I felt, the desire to contribute and pull my weight as a newlywed husband, and the frustration of not yet finding my place in the professional world. Long nights at a data center and an unsettling encounter with authority set the stage for an unexpected breakthrough: securing a mathematician position at the Defense Mapping Agency. This twist was a turning point that changed everything.

From unraveling the intricacies of programming languages to pioneering advancements in digital cartography, I chased discovery with relentless passion. But growth didn't come without challenges. Transitioning into leadership meant confronting the human side of progress—performance disputes, tough decisions, and the weight of job cuts. These moments tested me, but they also taught me the power of empathy and clear communication in leading meaningful change.

Part II isn't just about the work I did—it's about adapting to uncertainty and finding opportunities where none seemed to exist. It's about learning, taking risks, and never shying away from the unknown. Ultimately, it's a powerful illustration of resilience, the belief in the possibility of finding purpose, and the transformative power of service, even in the face of adversity.

CHAPTER 3

FROM NIGHT SHIFTS TO NEW HORIZONS

"The only way to do great work is to love what you do."
—STEVE JOBS

Navigating unemployment and an unsettling experience with the National Security Agency (NSA) tested my resolve, but it also fueled my determination to find a career that aligned with my passions and values. This chapter explores the challenges of early adulthood and the search for meaningful work.

When	1976	1977
Rank	Graduation, Marriage, Data Center, NSA	GS-5
Location	Lebanon, Illinois	DMAAC (St. Louis)

A POSTGRAD LEAP INTO ADULTHOOD

I graduated from college in May 1976 and got married in June. Unemployed but enjoying the early days of married life, I felt the urgency to find a job quickly. Luckily, I was able to rent a tiny hovel of a house from my father for only seventy-five dollars a month, which relieved some of the financial pressure. Still, the clock was ticking to establish a solid financial footing. My wife had made a career in teaching, and I was determined to contribute and avoid sinking into idleness. Out of necessity, I landed a night-shift job at a private-sector data center in St. Louis.

The situation wasn't ideal. Our schedules clashed completely. I worked late under the cold glow of fluorescent lights and CRT screens, finally stumbling into bed before dawn, a few hours before my wife woke to start her day. The conflicting hours were not conducive to connubial bliss, but we needed the paychecks.

Each evening, after an early dinner, I climbed into my 1969 Chevy and drove out on Interstate 70, the evening sun blazing orange beyond the Poplar Street Bridge over the Mississippi. With the top down, the wind whipped through my hair, carrying the tang of river water and the acrid bite of smoke from nearby chemical plants. The Corvair's flat-six engine, situated in the rear, sputtered and smoked behind me like an old friend. A quirky vehicle that I had worked on alongside my dad, the car had its faults, but I adored every bit of its weird charm. To me, it was freedom on wheels. To Ralph Nader's *Unsafe at Any Speed* I'd scoff, "Catch me if you can!" It was my ticket to a new chapter in life.

NIGHT SHIFT AT THE DATA CENTER

The data center sat on the edge of St. Louis, its dull exterior blind to the hum of technological life within. Inside, the air hung cold and stale, heavy with the scent of ozone and hot circuits. The guard at the front desk gave me an annoying smile.

"You must be the new guy. Good luck," he said, with a chuckle that made me uneasy. I stepped into the mainframe room, the door closing behind me with a definitive thud. The room was large, dominated by rows of IBM System/360 mainframes and peripherals. Their towering cabinets blinked with tiny lights. Tape drives whirred like mechanical heartbeats. Boxes of punch cards and printout paper were stacked everywhere, nestled beside cabinets lined with rows of white three-ring binders. Each binder held step-by-step instructions detailing how to run the software applications for our shift, a structured roadmap in a sea of organized chaos.

There were only three other operators that night, all dressed in 1970s fashion: flared pants, polyester shirts, long hair, and sideburns. They glanced at me, sharing smirks that said it all. I was the rookie, clueless and green. The system manager barely acknowledged me. Engrossed in his console, a lanky figure in his thirties, his long hair and beard gave him a classic '70s techie look.

"Take that desk," one operator instructed, jerking his thumb.

Nervously, I sat down at my station, looked around, and took in the rhythmic hum of the machines that surrounded me. My fingers hesitated over the keyboard, knowing this world demanded perfection. I had to abide by the unspoken rule: *prove yourself or be swallowed by the night.* As I took my seat in front of the roll-and-scroll console, the thrum of tape drives and chatter of printouts created a soothing background noise that lulled the world outside into oblivion. This was the beginning of my journey through the heart of the computer revolution, a time dominated by large mainframe computers that dictated the work environment with their physical presence. Unlike the sleek, virtual world of modern computing that would come decades later, 1970s computing was a tactile, heavy-lifting affair. Input came in the form of boxes of neatly stacked punch cards, while output was delivered in endless reams of printout paper. I spent hours sorting through and preparing punch card decks for processing, only to be rewarded with massive printouts that further filled the crowded space in the data center. The paper itself was deadly. If the system didn't manage to frustrate you, the paper cuts would. Forget digital headaches; my battle scars were strictly analog.

HIGH STAKES AND HEX DUMPS

The massive, expensive mainframes were indispensable for handling critical operations like payroll, inventory management, and financial processing. At our data center, we offered a time-sharing model, leasing out our computing power to companies in need of reliable software solutions and time on our mainframes. This was high-stakes work. If a software program stopped working or crashed during its nightly run, businesses relying on our services would face dire consequences. The pressure to perform was real, and unchecked failure was not an option. My job was to keep those programs running, and I monitored them like a vigilant night nurse. When they failed, I became the doctor charged with getting them back up as soon as possible.

On the job, I quickly learned the critical skill of diagnosing the cause of a program that crashed. When a software program quit unexpectedly on our mainframe, the last thing it would do before going silent was "vomit" and print out page after page of seemingly incomprehensible hexadecimal gibberish called a hex dump. Diagnosing the cause of the crash involved pouring over these dumps. My task was to decipher the reason for the crash, which was no easy feat considering the sheer volume and complexity of each dump. But just like the quadratic equations that I loved to solve at night with my father at our kitchen table, the exact cause of that computer crash was somewhere in the three-inch-thick pile of paper printout filled with hexadecimal characters. My job was to find the broken needle in that haystack, fix the needle, and sew the program's operation back together. But first, I had to find the needle.

LEARNING THE LANGUAGE OF MACHINES

To better understand the logic behind the software programs operating in the data center, I taught myself COBOL (Common Business Oriented Language) and IBM Job Control Language, or JCL. Mastering COBOL and JCL gave me a whole new set of mental tools, much like adding a power drill and saw to my home handyman tool kit. Hex dumps were like X-rays to me. I could peer into the inner workings of the IBM 360 and decipher even the most cryptic code. If the problem that caused the crash was a simple typo or a misplaced punch card, I would fix it and restart the program.

Occasionally, the errors were beyond my authority to resolve. Even when I had pinpointed the bug, this meant I had no choice but to call the programmers who had written the software, dragging them out of bed to come in and fix their faulty programming.

They hated getting that dreaded 2:30 a.m. phone call as much as I hated making it, yet, I always thought to myself, if this were my code, I would WANT that late-night telephone call, because I'd be embarrassed that something I wrote didn't run as it should.

The operational intricacy of the IBM 360 was like learning a whole new way of thinking. Each moment in that data center, illuminated in the green CRT glow, reinforced my technical abilities. I developed a knack for troubleshooting, for recognizing patterns hidden in chaos, and for handling challenges with confidence and calm determination. I learned to shuffle stacks of eighty-column punch cards with the finesse of a Las Vegas card shark and sniff out data errors like a bloodhound on steroids.

MORE THAN A JOB

In those late-night hours surrounded by humming machines, I had plenty of time to think, uncovering insights about who I was and what I wanted. I discovered a surprising strength in recognizing patterns and a determination to find order amid chaos. Whether it was in hex dumps or mathematical equations, I relished the challenge of cracking the puzzle. Along the way, I developed a genuine affinity for computer languages. Learning COBOL and JCL became more than just a skillset; it opened up a powerful new way to analyze and solve problems.

And through it all, I realized something even more profound. I wanted a career, not just a paycheck. The data center, for all its merits, felt static. I couldn't see a clear path of growth, and I longed for a role where my contributions could scale larger, with greater impact, and where my work could offer opportunities for advancement and meaning.

Looking back, those nights were transformational. They guided me to recognize my strengths, clarified the path I wanted to pursue in my career, and gave me the technical foundation that underpinned my professional future. Every program fixed, every line of code untangled, and every error resolved was a step closer to building the version of myself that I was meant to become. Meanwhile, since I had a college degree in mathematics, a rudimentary grasp of civil service, and a strong desire to find a day job with career potential, I applied for a government civil service job through an open, continuous vacancy announcement. This type of posting allows the government to recruit qualified candidates on an ongoing basis for positions with persistent vacancies, as they often struggle to fill these roles.

NATIONAL SECURITY AGENCY AND THE CASTING COUCH

Through my application, I caught the attention of the National Security Agency, the NSA, at Fort Meade, Maryland, and soon received an invitation to interview at their headquarters. They were intrigued by my mathematical and pattern-finding skills, and they wanted to evaluate whether I had the right stuff for code breaking. The invitation filled me with excitement and nervous energy. The NSA was shrouded in secrecy and prestige; this opportunity felt like a monumental step forward.

The level of the offered position was a GS-12! I was astonished. A GS-12 was the same GS level as my father at the time! I never imagined it possible that I could *start* my career at the same level my father had reached after years of effort. Yet, as excited as I was, the downside realities began to weigh on my mind. Moving to Washington, DC, would mean leaving behind everything familiar—friends, families, home, and community—for a future filled with uncertainty. The thought was daunting. Despite the unknowns and the sacrifices it demanded, I resolved to weigh the opportunity with an open mind, knowing it could be a step worth taking.

After making my way to Fort Meade, the day of testing and interviews unfolded as I worked through an intense series of evaluations designed to gauge my aptitude for computational and analytical thinking. At first, I felt a surge of pride just being a part of such a thorough process. The experience validated the talents I knew I had. However, as the day progressed, something unexpected overshadowed the experience. During one of the testing sessions, a male employee who was overseeing part of the process made an unwelcome sexual advance toward me. He offered to help me pass the test in exchange for something personal, a proposition that left me stunned. The setting amplified the unsettling nature of the advance. This was the NSA, an institution that required abiding trust and professionalism. Yet, here I was, facing someone who misused their power for personal gain. At the time, homosexuality was considered a security risk and a disqualifying condition for employment. The rationale was that those in same-sex relationships would be susceptible to blackmail. This policy made the advance all the more baffling. I was straight and rejected the proposition outright. But in rejecting it, I was acutely aware of the precariousness of my position. He had the power over my future at NSA, and I had none.

The interview process left a lasting scar, not solely because it revealed an abuse of power, but because it shattered my belief in the fairness of the system. What should have been a moment of pride became a sobering lesson in vulnerability, as I realized that my intellect, confidence, and trust in the system were powerless against someone who was positioned and adept at manipulating the machinery of bureaucracy for personal gain.

This encounter became a turning point that shattered the allure the NSA once held for me. Regardless of the prestige of the agency, I couldn't see myself thriving within an environment where such behavior could occur, especially not in a setting that demanded integrity above all else. I returned home deeply disappointed and continued my search for a career elsewhere. From that experience, I gained profound insights about the reality of power dynamics. I saw how the misuse of authority could corrode even the most respected institutions, and being in a powerless position showed me just how easily respect could be lost. At the same time, I developed a renewed sense of self-worth. No role, no matter how appealing, was worth compromising my integrity.

ANSWERED PRAYERS

Prayers answered! One otherwise ordinary afternoon, tucked between restless hope and relentless uncertainty, a letter from the Defense Mapping Agency Aerospace Center (DMAAC) arrived. The envelope held the culmination of everything I'd been striving for. I'd been selected to work at DMAAC, in a St. Louis facility, as a GS-5 mathematician, with a salary of $8,995 per year. Relief washed over me, as if a weight I hadn't realized I was carrying had been lifted, making way for hope and excitement.

St. Louis was just twenty miles away, close enough to feel comfortably connected to home. I'd get to leverage the foundation of my math degree while stepping into a meaningful role. This was more than a job offer. The moment felt like validation, proof that persistence could lead to something tangible. I clutched the letter tightly, reading it over and over, scarcely believing that both my education and location had aligned so perfectly with this opportunity. For the first time in months, I allowed myself to imagine more than just surviving. This was stability, professional purpose, and growth, wrapped into one solid step forward. Whispering aloud, I couldn't contain my excitement, "Sierra Hotel!"—Air Force slang for *Mission Accomplished*.

A CHOICE TO MAKE

And yet, doubt lingered. Should I take the stable path of government service or reach for the flashier prospects my friends were chasing in the private sector? It felt like the classic dilemma, a bird in the hand or the two in the bush. The pressure was real. Friends of mine were pursuing roles in finance and consulting, dazzled by the potential of bonuses, nice offices, and admiration from peers. And some of my family didn't hide their disappointment. To them, a government job was settling, a choice lacking ambition. "Why aim so low when the world is offering more?" their skepticism more than hinting at the tired stereotype about lazy government employees. Even I couldn't help but question if I was limiting myself, or worse, selling myself short.

STAYING THE COURSE

But in those moments of doubt, my grandmother's voice echoed in my mind, strong and steady, much like the woman herself. "You're like a train on a track. No matter the obstacles, if you stay the course, you'll reach your destination. Good things lie ahead, so trust in your efforts and know that there's light at the end of the tunnel." She had been a nurse who understood the quiet satisfaction of vocation, of contributing to something greater. Her words weren't loud or commanding, but they lingered like a constant undercurrent, reminding me that a life built on purpose and persistence could be just as rewarding, if not more so, than one purely chasing wealth.

That clarity sharpened my resolve. With her wisdom in mind, I made my decision. I accepted the offer at DMAAC. The weeks of underemployed uncertainty that accompanied my data center job and the nights of introspection after the unsettling NSA experience were over.

The offer letter was a passport to stability, a door to endless possibilities, and proof that I could carve out a future uniquely my own. I was ready to grow, to learn, to contribute. And so, with quiet conviction and a heart full of hope, I whispered to myself once more, "Sierra Hotel." St. Louis, here I come!

CARTOGRAPHY CLASS

My introduction to the Defense Mapping Agency Aerospace Center began at their St. Louis South Annex facility at 8900 South Broadway, *8900* for short, where every recruit completed a two-week orientation known as Carto Class. This was my first taste of life as a real civil servant, and it was eye-opening. New employees learned about cartography and tried their hands at using a stereoplotter and other cartographic equipment. The class introduced newly hired employees to production methods for the hard copy and digital products produced by DMAAC for use by the Air Force.

Excited and curious, I pulled into the parking lot at 8900. The long, low green building was nondescript from the outside, but I knew that inside lay the challenges of a career in civil service introduced to me through a world of cartography, mathematics, and mapmaking production. I carried my letter of employment and a few pencils in a manila envelope under my arm. Entering the building, I was greeted by a friendly face, handed a folder with some reading material, and told to take a seat in the waiting area. Before long, the carto class instructor welcomed me and thirteen other recruits. He explained why we were there and what we would learn over the next few weeks. We all stood around the periphery of the room, chatting and waiting for class to begin. My eyes scanned the group, searching for other mathematicians, seeking a basis of commonality and camaraderie.

THE STEREOPLOTTER

The walls of the classroom were adorned with diagrams and charts illustrating various cartographic products and techniques of orthophotography and stereoscopic photogrammetry. The large room contained enough chairs for each member of our class and was otherwise filled with various cartography and mensuration machines. As we sipped on old coffee, our instructor walked us through the basics of mapmaking and what DMAAC did, from the principles of projection to the science and machinery of photogrammetry. We were invited to try out a stereoplotter, a contraption that looked somewhat like something out of a science fiction movie—basically an advanced version of those old 3D View-Master toys we played with as kids. The stereoplotter used stereo photographs to determine elevations and map contour lines. While I was standing there watching, a fellow student, a cartography major, leaned over and whispered under his breath, "Be careful; if you get too good at that job, you'll never leave it. Strong galley slaves never go free until the ship goes down."

He was right. That job meant endless shift work in a cold, gloomy room, glued to a set of eyepieces for hours at a time. Both feet had to dance on pedals while your hands wrangled knobs, and your eyes? They weren't going anywhere except straight into your soul, begging for coffee breaks that would never come. Taken aback and now, on my guard, I made a mental note to avoid the stereoplotter and all it entailed.

UNDERSTANDING THE "WHY"

I wondered what I was doing there. I was a mathematician, not a mapmaker. The class seemed to be tailored for cartographers in training, and I felt like a square peg in a room full of round holes, a misfit trying to find my place among the precision tools and meticulously designed maps that seemed to have no use for my skills. But the experience taught me a valuable lesson that stayed with me throughout my career: Understanding the *why* is the first and most crucial step in any new task. Before people can commit to the *what*, they need to have a clear grasp of an organization's *purpose*. It's why even a McDonald's floor sweeper knows they're contributing to an environment where customers feel welcome to buy hamburgers.

The cartography class may have been a hands-on introduction to the tools and processes of mapmaking, but it also offered a subtle glimpse into the why behind it all, providing a foundation for seeing the bigger picture and how everything connected. As class ended, I felt eager to dive deeper into the math that drove the world of cartography. That carto class had been literally an eye-opening experience. I knew this was just the beginning of my journey through the bureaucracy of civil service and the missions of the Defense Mapping Agency and the Department of Defense. Through that experience, I came to understand the importance of context and how essential it is to consider the bigger picture. I also realized the value of stepping into uncharted territory, even when things don't make perfect sense at first.

CLASS IS OVER. GET TO WORK.

The main Defense Mapping Agency Aerospace Center production campus was located in refurbished buildings of the old St. Louis Arsenal, a relic from a bygone era. The map factory campus was shoehorned into a few acres of land occupied by brick and limestone buildings, dating back to the Civil War. Back then, it supplied guns and ammunition to the Union Army during the War Between the States. Now, the same buildings held secrets of their own: methods to collect data about everything on Earth, then convert that information into maps, charts, and digital products to support the mission of the US Air Force and the Department of Defense.

The DMAAC compound at the arsenal was nestled between two prominent St. Louis landmarks: the Anheuser-Busch Brewery to the west and the Mississippi River to the east. The beer brewery sat on a hill with an imposing red brick facade with chimneys rising high into the air like sentinels guarding the south side of the city. With every westerly breeze, a thick, yeasty aroma of mashed fermenting hops, working to change sweet wort into the King of Beers, wafted down the hill to blanket the Arsenal.

The mapping compound was bounded to the east by the Mississippi. The river's tranquil beauty and muddy banks offered a soothing contrast to the hustle and bustle of the city. But that peaceful setting belied a deceptively raw power. After heavy rains or snowmelt in the north, the rising river would send its water upstream, pushing sewage back up through the drains and into the ancient basements of these buildings.

A NEW BEGINNING

When I found my way to Building 36 and the mathematical support branch office, I felt excited and proud of my new position—a math grad with a professional mathematician position. My supervisor was a tall man with the eyes and mannerisms of Morgan Freeman—articulate, experienced, good natured and very, very smart. He met me with a smile and a sincere handshake, and I could tell he'd welcomed many new employees before me. Yet he made me feel special and welcome. Not only did he know his business, but he knew the larger bureaucratic dynamics of DMAAC and how to work with them. Standing there, poised at the precipice of a civil service career, I was gripped by a torrent of emotions, eager to tackle problems and opportunities I had never seen before. Yet, alongside the exhilaration, I couldn't ignore my palpable nervousness. I was comfortable and confident about taking on new challenges, but I also felt the gnawing apprehension at the thought of falling short on as yet unknown standards of expectations for my job performance. This was my first big job out of college, and I didn't know what *good* looked like.

THE IBM 1620

Specifically, I served as a mathematician for the mathematical support branch, responsible for performing a variety of mathematical analyses in support of DMAAC production operations. The room where I was to fulfill that role was dimly lit by a bluish-white glow from overhead hanging fluorescent lights that cast gray shadows across the desktops. Cool and slightly humid air blew out of air vents from the building's noisy air conditioning system, fighting a losing battle to keep out moisture from the mighty Mississippi River, a mere six hundred feet beyond the walls. The large, gray brick-lined room was quiet except for the occasional cacophony of a lone keypunch machine and the steady hum of a sleeping hulk of an ancient computer.

The IBM 1620 was the size of a compact car. This behemoth was an embodiment of the power and limited precision of mid-century computing. The massive machine's metallic frame, adorned with rows of toggle switches and knobs, loomed over the room like an ancient idol. Its console lights blinked and demanded to be served a sacrifice of eighty-column punch cards, which were swallowed by a hungry maw of an adjoining card reader with menacing perforated teeth. After quiet and due consideration, the offering's fate was adjudicated, finally revealed by this staccato sound of an electric typewriter console rack. *Tacka-tacka*, silence. *Racka*, silence. *Racka-tacka-tacka...* Spewing out answers eagerly sought, or coldly announcing errors easily made from faulty logic in the cards. This electronic idol was a benign but finicky master. It would consume as many stacks of punch cards as a humble human could feed it, never getting its fill. However, the machine had a taste for perfection. If any card had the tiniest defect, such as a keypunch hole mis-centered by a millimeter, the monstrous deity would spit out the card, stop its operation, and demand you return to the keypunch to correct your stupid mortal error.

THE CHALLENGE

Ten metal desks cluttered with maps, calculators, papers, books, punch cards, and copies of the day's newspaper surrounded the mighty beast, providing workspace for our mathematician brains to meticulously encode our thoughts onto those eighty-column cards of FORTRAN (FORmula TRANslation) software code. In this room, amid the clatter and whir of that electronic, mechanical mind, we mathematicians sought harmony between the accuracy of our equations and the beauty of the Earth. On these desks, naked mathematics modeled a clothed world. Bits fought art. Engineered precision wrestled with cartographic aesthetics. Computer automation fought human labor.

Ultimately, automation would win.

Our supervisor created a friendly competition between me and two other newly hired mathematicians. We were tasked with writing the most efficient FORTRAN program for finding the shortest path between two points on a three-dimensional ellipsoid. The prize was bragging rights. Whoever achieved a clean compilation and the correct answer printed out by the IBM 1620 would be declared the winner.

I took a creative approach by mathematically spinning the ellipsoid so the arc of the path lay flat in two dimensions. Imagine the 3D form flattened on a table. This way, I could easily solve the problem using known formulas to determine the length of the arc. Thanks to having learned COBOL at the time-sharing data center, I picked up FORTRAN in no time. Coupled with my punch card slinging skills, I ran circles around my colleagues and, ultimately, solved the problem to win those bragging rights.

A BUREAUCRATIC FREIGHT TRAIN

A few months into my job, bureaucracy hit me like a freight train when I received a directive from my branch chief ordering me to train a new GS-7 employee, despite me being in a lower pay grade level, a GS-5. The irony was clear: This person, on his first day in the job, would earn more than me while learning from me, only to eventually become my supervisor! Frustrated and unsure what to do, I mustered the courage to discuss the situation with my supervisor.

It wasn't an easy step. I didn't even know if raising the issue was the right thing to do, nor what my supervisor could realistically do about it. Still, I felt compelled to speak up. To his credit, my supervisor listened carefully and acknowledged the unfairness of the situation, but his hands were tied. There was nothing he could do. That conversation, though validating, left me deflated and also illuminated a harsh truth. The system's policies often tied the hands of even those in positions of authority.

LEARNING TO NAVIGATE

With no other recourse, I turned to the act of writing a memorandum for record, an MFR, which is a bureaucratic ritual that accomplished nothing tangible but allowed me a faint sense of closure. I had arrived at this job eager to prove myself. My role was to perform mathematical analyses and computations to support production operations. Although the technical challenges proved rewarding, I quickly observed that success in civil service demanded more than expertise. Mastering the management of bureaucracy became equally important.

This experience taught me a lesson about the nature of bureaucracy in civil service. Like gravity, it was an omnipresent, unavoidable force that required navigation rather than resistance. To succeed, I needed to find a balance between pursuing the organization's mission and navigating its bureaucratic underpinnings, transforming the latter into a tool that served my goals rather than an obstacle that hindered me.

I came to understand that the key was not to resist bureaucracy, but to learn about it and adapt to it. To move forward, I had to balance my dedication to the organization's mission with the skill of navigating the system's labyrinthine rules. Reminded of my dad's advice (*if a part doesn't fit, turn it upside down and try it again*), I began to see bureaucracy not as a fixed obstacle but as something that could be shaped and used as a tool to help me reach my goals and progress within the constraints it imposed on success in civil service. I began to understand that my future success required both technical excellence and the adaptability to work within the power structures that shaped the organization.

CHAPTER 4

FROM ELEVATION TO INNOVATION

A DIGITAL REVOLUTION

"The greatest danger for most of us is not that our aim is too high and we miss it, but that it is too low and we reach it."

—MICHELANGELO

My time at the Defense Mapping Agency was marked by a passion for innovation and a desire to push the boundaries of technology. This chapter chronicles my early breakthroughs in digital cartography and the challenges of championing new ideas within a traditional organization.

When	1977	1980		1982	1984		1986
Rank	GS-7	GS-9	GS-11	GS-12	GS-13	GS-14	GS-15
Location	DMAAC (St. Louis)				DMA/SPOEM (DC)		

CODE MEETS CARTOGRAPHY

Software programming, for me, has always been a craft, a journey of discovery and creation. By the early 1980s, my craft had developed into something far more precise and technical than I could have initially imagined. My coding toolbox had grown significantly: FORTRAN was like a second language, COBOL and JCL felt like dependable business partners, and Assembly language served as my tiny screwdriver to fine-tune the smallest mechanisms in the world of code. FORTH (the programming language) was my jet pack, fast and nimble for creating graphics prototypes, while BASIC (Beginner's All-purpose Symbolic Instruction Code) was my digital box of LEGOs, perfect for piecing together ideas on my home Commodore 64 microcomputer.

Together, these skills provided me with an incredible sense of expression, the power to shape and mold the digital realm, and that was nothing short of exhilarating, like being a writer fluent in multiple languages, each one offering just the right words and nuances to craft the perfect story.

CARTOGRAPHER, PROGRAMMER, AND PROBLEM-SOLVER

Even though I was reassigned to a position of "Cartographer," my job and passion was software programming. I honed my programming skills and was introduced to the fascinating world of data structures and databases that the Defense Mapping Agency (DMA) used to describe the Earth's surface. I knew about geography, just like everybody knows about latitude and longitudes. In this job, I learned the data structures and algorithms used to represent everything you see on a map.

My role as an applications programmer in the Computer Division's Applications Programming branch was rooted in the intricate mathematics of Earth's elevations, slopes, features, lines of sight, and vertical obstructions. I was tasked with deriving, developing, analyzing, and coding complex mathematical algorithms for analytical triangulation, terrain contour matching, and matrix generation. This also included handling digital terrain elevation data, digital feature analysis, and vertical obstruction data. The US Air Force was the Aerospace Center's primary customer, and it was obvious why they relied on precise Earth elevation and vertical obstruction data, alongside the essential maps and charts, for their missions. My skills and contributions were recognized, and I steadily climbed the ranks, rising from GS-7 to GS-9, then to GS-11, and finally to GS-12.

THE RISE OF THE MINICOMPUTER

The 1980s also marked a pivotal moment in technological advancement for computer-aided cartography, as DMA began incorporating minicomputers into its production processes. DMA's computing ecosystem, primarily comprising UNIVAC (Universal Automatic Computer) mainframes, was being augmented with minicomputers. With their small size and relatively low cost, these machines were well-suited to handle complex tasks required for computer-aided mapping production.

Integrating minicomputers with cartography machines was like adding an electric pedal-assist to a bicycle, enabling riders (cartographers) to tackle daunting hills and distances while the rider controlled the route. The widespread availability of minicomputers at DMAAC became my digital workshop, brimming with opportunities for exploration and discovery. Minicomputers like Digital Equipment Corporation's PDP-8s and 11s; Modular Computer Systems' MODCOMP IIIs; and my favorite, the Data General NOVA, a 16-bit minicomputer about the size of today's desktop PC, opened up a world of possibilities.

DECODING THE EARTH

At the time, my world was more than writing code; it was about decoding the Earth itself. My projects revolved around cartographic data, something most people probably don't think too much about, but which was crucial in so many ways.

I was fascinated by the way terrain data could translate into something visual, something real. I honed this passion and became immersed in the mathematics behind it all—slope, lines of sight, vertical obstructions, and the Earth's surface elevation points. Digital Terrain Elevation Data (DTED) became my biggest obsession. Imagine, if you will, a grid of points stretching across a map, like a huge pincushion, each one representing a precise elevation. Together, they formed a digital model of the Earth's surface, and programming became the key to turning those raw data points into something we could display and understand.

I was in my element, like a fish in water, programming the brains behind the map and fully immersed in a unique mix of geography, mathematics, software development, and a growing fascination with computer graphics. This period led to my first significant breakthrough, marking the start of an exciting new chapter in my career.

THE DATA TAPES

In the early '80s, the primary digital storage devices were not hard drives; rather, we used reels of magnetic tape about the size of an inch-thick dinner plate. DMA had vast libraries filled with these magnetic tapes, which stored their inventory of cartographic knowledge. All the tapes looked the same, except for a unique identification number written on a label attached to the case that stored the tape. The problem was that you couldn't tell what geographic data was stored on the tape by looking at the number on the case.

A mix-up could cause chaos. For example, what if the Air Force asked for terrain data around the Miami airport and DMAAC shipped them a magnetic tape of data over Denver instead? A mistake like that could jeopardize a military operation.

That problem became my mission.

A MENTOR'S GUIDANCE

I was lucky enough to work with a brilliant and inspirational advisor. This leader, with his quick wit and sharp intellect, was the mentor I never knew I needed when it came to tech. The man had a knack for explaining complex concepts in a way that made them click, like puzzle pieces falling into place. He was gifted at solving the toughest problems, inventing clever storage solutions at the time when a ten-megabyte disk drive was the size of a trash can lid.

But what I'll always be grateful for is the powerful development environment he set up, a sandbox of humming computers and blinking lights where I could truly run free. This was a playground for the mind, stocked with all the hardware and software needed to explore graphics systems, computer languages, and input/output protocols. My mentor gave me the keys, both literally and figuratively, and said, "Go explore." And explore, I did.

Hours melted away as I delved into programming languages and graphics cards, and dissected comm boards to see how they ticked. I dreamed about LIFO (Last In, First Out) queues and talked in my sleep about recursive routines, waking up eager to run to the computer each morning and test them out.

My advisor was always there, a guiding presence, offering ideas and encouragement, answering questions, and occasionally dropping by with a new challenge to tackle. That lab, and that advisor's unshakable belief in me, became the bedrock upon which I built every subsequent technical achievement.

THE IMAGE MANIPULATION STATION

Collaborating with my mentor and another coder, we developed the Image Manipulation Station (IMS), a pioneering system and DMA's first online digital display and validation system. IMS revolutionized how DMA worked with terrain elevation data, providing a real-time graphic display of this data, allowing analysts to validate and modify it interactively before it was distributed to users like the Air Force. This significantly improved the accuracy and efficiency of the mapmaking process.

Then, I took it a step further by blending a standard contour gray level representation of elevation data with terrain slope to generate a color-shaded relief visualization of the digital terrain data. This enabled quality control analysts to view the tape's elevation matrices on color graphics monitors.

For the first time, analysts could see a topographic color-shaded relief display of the data from the tape that looked like a paper map. This innovation vividly revealed topographic details such as mountain shadows, valleys, hills, and the flat expanses of rivers, lakes, and oceans. By comparing the image on the computer monitor to a paper map of the same area, it was easy to verify that the data on the magnetic tape was or was not the geographic area requested by an Air Force customer.

HUMANIZING THE INTERFACE

The IMS offered more than just realistic visuals, bringing about a significant shift in how cartographers and analysts engaged with computer systems. At that time, accessing data on DMA computers required a specific set of skills. Cartographers had to use complex computer query languages unique to each specific system, or they had to know and type in the commands that the cartographic machines accepted. It was as if only the "high priests" of computing who properly created queries with hieroglyphics could access the sacred information.

This barrier frustrated me. Why should information be locked away from all but a select few? Why should someone who simply needed data for their work be required to master a complicated language or command line interface to access it? I believed computers should serve users, not the other way around.

This philosophy carried through to the IMS. I was determined to create an interface that was straightforward and easy to use, built on a numbered menu-pick system. No cryptic languages or intimidating commands, just a simple design that allowed anyone to use it. This commitment to human-centered design (HCD) shaped not only the IMS but also became a defining element of my career, reemerging later in my work at the Department of Veterans Affairs, but it had its roots here, in these early DMA projects.

BEYOND STAND-ALONE SYSTEMS

While working on new ways to visualize mapping, charting, and geodesy data, I used my skills in Assembly language to push boundaries in computer-to-computer communications. Back then, DMA's computing ecosystem was a patchwork of stand-alone machines from different manufacturers, which made data exchange between systems a challenge. Transferring information usually required physically transporting magnetic tapes from one computer to another, like passing handwritten notes across a busy classroom. But this method came with its own risks. Tapes could be misplaced, damaged, or even rendered unreadable, causing headaches and delays in the production pipeline.

I spent many late nights poring over technical manuals and chipping away at the Assembly language code to write digital communications protocols necessary for remote minicomputers to talk to the DMA mainframes. This integration eliminated the need to carry tapes around when a relatively small amount of data needed to be transferred from one computer to another. The knowledge I gained in this process, down to the bit level, would pay huge dividends later in my career.

A TIE, A CHOICE, A TRANSFORMATION

One morning, while getting ready for my usual commute, I paused in front of my closet. An unexpected whim surfaced, breaking through the monotony. My eyes settled on a tie—a simple, navy-blue tie that had hung there for ages, untouched and overlooked. Why not wear it today? Not for anyone, not to "dress for success," not for a special event, but simply to shake things up and see how it felt. I wrapped it around my neck, adjusted the knot until it looked about right, and with a final firm pull, stepped out to face the day.

A SHIFT IN PERCEPTION

Walking into the office, I sensed the shift before anyone said a word. Heads turned. Conversations hushed. The usual chorus of "Morning" felt stilted and mechanical. As I walked down the hallway to my cubicle, coworkers stared. I thought nothing of it at first. Why would I? It was only a tie. But as the hours crawled by, the weight of their gazes settled on me like a stone.

The usual chitchat was replaced by unusual silence, and the familiar camaraderie that characterized those Midwestern mornings had vanished, replaced by an unspoken unease that hung in the air like a fog. My buddies from the after-work softball league barely nodded at me. My lunchtime chess companion remarked, "Looking sharp today." Was it praise or suspicion?

The tie, it turned out, carried more weight than I could have anticipated. To them, it didn't look like a simple accessory or a mere change in routine. It was a statement. They saw less of me in that moment and more of what the tie represented. Authority. Status. Ambition. Management.

Whispers floated through the office like loose threads. I heard snatches of conversations as I passed. "Wonder who he's trying to impress?" "Going 'corporate'?"

A SYMBOL OF CHOICE

I retreated to my desk to bury myself in software, but I couldn't shake the undercurrent of unease. The clack of keyboards and muted phone calls around me felt distant. I admit, it was a little weird to see a tie hanging down from my neck when I looked at my keyboard. Now it felt heavy. I tugged at it, wondering how such a minor thing could wield such a staggering influence. It had morphed into something much bigger than a piece of cloth.

It sparked tension, shifted perceptions, and drew invisible lines between me and my coworkers.

A tie. To them, it meant betrayal. To me, it meant choice. And at that moment, I decided I would wear it again the next day, and the day after that. In that seemingly insignificant choice of apparel, I claimed ownership of who I was and who I wanted to become, refusing to be boxed in by others' expectations. Going forward, I would own it, tie and all.

WHEN OPPORTUNITY KNOCKED

The tie was just the beginning, a seemingly trivial act laden with extraordinary weight. The choice wasn't about fabric or fashion; the act served as a declaration, a quiet rebellion against the expectations of others. To them, a tie symbolized a different conformity, perhaps even betrayal. For me, the tie became a symbol of an assertion of ownership over who I was and who I wanted to become.

That small act lit a fire deep within me, a flame fueled by purpose and unshakable resolve. Each decision I made afterward burned brighter, guiding me toward a path I was only beginning to glimpse, leading me straight to my next moment of reckoning.

I had heard whispers of a new special program office being created, tasked with harnessing cutting-edge technology. Its mission? Nothing short of revolution. The goal was to develop state-of-the-art digital cartographic production systems, allowing for faster and more accurate map creation based on digital imagery. The precision, speed, and efficiency of these proposed systems would forever change how we understood and represented the world. It was ambitious. Bold. Daring. Innovative. Everything about it called to me, demanding my involvement. I could feel it. I wanted to be part of this.

My pulse quickened a little every time I thought about it. I knew I had the skills. I knew I had the passion. But opportunities like this didn't just land in your lap. You had to chase them down. You had to fight for them. And I was ready.

THE ENCOUNTER

It was a Thursday afternoon in February 1982, the kind of day that lulls you into thinking nothing extraordinary will happen. The office hummed quietly, the monotonous clacking of keyboards and the occasional ring of phones blending into a dull background. Cubicles stretched out in every direction, gray dividers hemming us into our own tiny worlds. Then came the noise—a growing commotion echoing down the hallway. Voices. Footsteps. The rhythm of something out of the ordinary.

I peered over the top of my cubicle and froze. There he was, walking confidently down the corridor. The leader of this new program, the force behind it. I recognized him immediately—the stories, the rumors, the whispered admiration. His presence was magnetic, commanding. Flanked by an entourage, he strode through the corridor like a ship cutting through waves. This was it. My chance.

My heart pounded as I scrambled out of my chair. Adrenaline surged through me, silencing every hesitation and doubt. Was I ready for this? Could I even pull this off? None of it mattered. If not now, when? I jogged to the hallway and stepped into his path.

"Sir," I said, sticking out my hand with more courage than I owned, "My name is Bill James. I am the best programmer in this building, and I want to work for you."

THE LEAP

I didn't recognize my own words. They were raw, unfiltered, powered by confidence I didn't know I had. The air thickened as his gaze locked onto mine. For a split second, time froze. And then, as if preordained, his answer sliced through the tension, sharp and rapid.

"Fine, start Monday in DC."

Monday? DC? The words slammed into me like a tidal wave. My mind reeled, grappling with the logistics. I had a job here. A home. A life in St. Louis, and he was asking me to pack it all up and move in a matter of days. But none of that mattered. The adrenaline coursing through me drowned out every doubt.

"Thank you, sir!" I blurted, my voice cracking with the mix of terror and triumph.

He didn't linger, already moving down the corridor with his entourage in tow. But I stood there, heart racing, as the weight of what had just happened fully sank in. I had done it. I had said the thing. Made the move. Put it all on the line. There was no turning back now.

I didn't technically start that Monday, of course, but I applied for the position, interviewed relentlessly, and positioned myself for success. A few months later, I moved to DC to take the job, leaving behind the familiar for something extraordinary.

The tie was just the beginning. This was the next stage in a story that was mine to write. And for the first time in a long time, I knew exactly where I was heading.

CLIMBING HIGHER, MOVING FASTER

By the early 1980s, the Defense Mapping Agency found itself at a crossroads. Long regarded as the world's premier mapmaking organization, it was clear that the traditional reliance on primarily manual, analog processes and hard copy source material was no longer sustainable. Advances in satellite remote sensing and the increasing complexity of military operations demanded a revolutionary shift in the way geospatial data and cartographic products were produced. The path forward was a daunting one—a full transition to digital processes was imperative to meet the military's growing demands for greater accuracy, speed, and adaptability. This pressing need marked the genesis of DMA's ambitious modernization effort, the Digital Production System (DPS), and it became a turning point for cartography.

At the heart of this revolution lay innovation, leadership, and the expertise of individuals dedicated to advancing the mission of the DMA. My involvement in this monumental transformation spanned key roles, each underscoring a commitment to breaking boundaries and bringing the agency's capabilities into a new era.

THE NEED FOR CHANGE

The driving force behind the Digital Production System was necessity. Military operations in the 1980s were heavily reliant on precision targeting and detailed simulations, both of which demanded data products with unprecedented fidelity. The analog systems at DMA, while groundbreaking in their prime, were showing their age. Production cycles often spanned years, and the ability to integrate new data or launch new products was limited by cumbersome manual processes.

Weapon systems, from terrain-following missiles to advanced simulators for mission rehearsals, required terrain data of the highest accuracy. The stakes were clear. Failure to modernize would put military operations at risk. The Hermann

Panel Report, sponsored by Congress and completed in 1982, concluded that DMA not only needed to expedite its modernization efforts but required entirely new systems that could handle digital source materials and automated processes.

This challenge was monumental. The Defense Mapping Agency needed to transform itself into a digital-first organization, capable of consolidating vast geospatial datasets, automating labor-intensive tasks, and delivering paper and digital mapping products with unmatched precision and timeliness. This transformation required operating at a scale and level of technical sophistication never before attempted by the Department of Defense.

MY ROLE IN THE REVOLUTION

From the outset, I embraced the opportunity to contribute to this historic undertaking. My initial involvement came as a program manager in the Special Program Office for Exploitation Modernization (SPOEM). I was responsible for leading the development and implementation of secure communication networks to support the digital production system. The focus was on ensuring that data could flow seamlessly between development contractors and DMA sites across the continental United States.

Coming from a sleepy town in Illinois, moving to DC was like stepping onto another planet. Everything was faster, bigger, and infinitely more expensive. The cost of a home nearly knocked me flat, but this was an opportunity that I knew was worth the sacrifice. I adjusted as quickly as I could, and from my first day in SPOEM, I gave it everything.

THE SPOEM OFFICE

The Special Program Office for Exploitation Modernization office building was situated in the heart of Northern Virginia, its exterior a plain, unassuming shell masking the brilliance within. Inside, the beige walls stretched around corners, their neutral tone offering little distraction to the sharp minds at work. The offices were arranged in a square around the floor, creating a continuous loop of workspaces. From these offices, wide windows framed outside scenes of ceaseless tides of traffic filtering through office buildings, banks, and restaurants.

The view was dynamic, almost hypnotic, as cars weaved in and out of congested parking lots and office workers bustled with purpose. To most, it was just the humdrum of suburban office life, yet to those within these walls, it was something more. The team here—PhDs, Senior Executives, engineers, analysts—saw patterns where others saw only chaos. They carried the weight of unparalleled expertise, their knowledge of mapmaking production so comprehensive, it often seemed otherworldly. This bustling panorama outside their windows was a silent partner in their work, a reminder of the complex systems they sought to organize and decode.

The square layout of the offices lent the floor a distinctive, almost circuit-like flow, as if mirroring the constant exchange of ideas among its occupants. Between the hushed corridors and evenly spaced doors, a quiet energy permeated the air borne of intellectual rigor and purpose. The faint aroma of coffee floated in the background, coupled with the occasional sound of pages flipping, keyboards clicking, or dry erase markers scrawling across whiteboards.

At the end of one hallway stood a large conference room, its presence commanding respect. Here, the most pivotal discussions took place. A long string of folding tables served as a main stage for heated debates, occasional paralysis by analysis, and bright moments of clarity that pushed the boundaries of what was thought possible. Papers were often spread across its surface in organized disarray, evidence of the relentless pursuit of innovation. The walls bore hastily sketched diagrams and specifications—pieces of puzzles that would come together in time.

Every corner of this floor radiated purpose. Conversations were clipped but meaningful, each exchange another piece in the complex machinery of their work. The windows offering views of the world below were a reminder of the stakes, the tangible systems and infrastructures influenced by their decisions. Outside, life carried on unbroken with the flow of pedestrians, the honk of impatient drivers, the steady hum of commerce. Both ordinary and extraordinary, a living, breathing backdrop to the precision unfolding within these walls.

This was far more than a traditional government office. The environment became a crucible for discovery, where some of the Agency's brightest minds transformed the chaos of the world into a sense of order. Here, ideas were born, refined, and sent out to reshape the bustling world endlessly visible just beyond the panes of glass.

SETTING EXPECTATIONS

After I settled into my office, my new boss called me in to welcome me aboard and share his expectations. They were enormous, made abundantly clear in one simple conversation. Leaning back in his chair, pausing for a few moments, the towering, down-to-earth figure said bluntly, "Welcome aboard. Let me be clear. If you screw up, I'll fire your ass!"

Without missing a beat, I responded, "Okay, but if I produce,

I want to be promoted without waiting for someone to die in front of me."

He smiled and said, "Deal." With a parting handshake, I knew this wouldn't be just a job; it was going to be a proving ground. And produce, I did. True to his word, my boss honored our deal, and the promotions came just as we had agreed.

SEGMENT PROGRAM MANAGER

As Segment Program Manager for communication systems, I held an important role in advancing the Defense Mapping Agency's capabilities by designing and implementing secure communication networks. These networks formed the initial backbone of the modernized production systems between DMA sites in the continental United States and facilitated intersite communications with development contractors. My responsibilities spanned technical, managerial, and strategic tasks, all aimed at delivering a future-ready communication infrastructure.

My role was a mix of technical expertise and strategic vision. I conducted in-depth analyses, defined system requirements, and managed vendor contracts to ensure performance. My early experience at DECCO, where I gained an understanding of DOD telecommunications lines, combined with my work at DMAAC, where I established intercomputer digital communication links, directly inspired my proposal to revolutionize intersite data transfers. I challenged the status quo method of shipping magnetic tapes via trucks by advocating for the adoption of dedicated 56 kilobits per second "long lines" communication pipes for data transfer. This vision, encapsulated in my semihumorous "Trucks Suck" proposal, replaced the outdated tape-shipping process with a modern, efficient point-to-point digital data transfer system, which offered a significant upgrade to DMA's operational capabilities. Later, as a Senior Systems Engineer, I applied this same drive to database management, leveraging a cutting-edge (at the time) client–server database architecture to create scalable and robust systems. These achievements demonstrated my knack for bridging the gap between abstract ideas and real-world solutions. Turning complex requirements into practical, impactful systems underscored my desire to drive impactful progress as part of DMA's modernization efforts.

TECHNOLOGICAL INNOVATION MEETS OPERATIONAL IMPACT

Implementing the DPS marked a leap forward for DMA. The modernization effort introduced digital soft copy techniques, automated cartographic functions, and centralized data storage systems—capabilities that had only been conceptualized previously. These innovations dramatically improved production speeds, cutting pipeline times from years to months, and in certain cases, weeks.

One revolutionary advancement was the system's ability to store geospatial data in a digital database, from which a wide variety of cartographic products could be generated. This flexibility enabled the tailoring of products to specific military needs, such as real-time situational maps for field commands or detailed terrain visualization for weapons guidance. The system also allowed for rapid updates, ensuring information provided to war-fighters was both current and actionable.

The road to modernization was not without its challenges. Transitioning from an analog production system to a fully digital one was, at times, an uphill battle against entrenched processes, bureaucratic organizational inertia, and technical uncertainty. When the program began in 1982, only about 10 percent of the required technology was commercially available. The rest had to be developed from scratch—a task that demanded coordination across contractors, government engineering teams, and DMA leadership.

A LEGACY OF TRANSFORMATION

The success of the Digital Production System defined an era of innovation at DMA and solidified its place as a pioneer in digital cartography. The system's capabilities set new standards for precision, efficiency, and adaptability in map production—a legacy that continues to influence geospatial systems used by the Department of Defense today.

Reflecting on my role in this endeavor, I am proud to have contributed to an effort that fundamentally changed the way the agency operated. My work ensured that pioneering concepts in communications, database management, and system architecture evolved from blueprints into reality. More importantly, it laid the foundation for a digital future, where geospatial intelligence became a decisive factor in military success.

The DPS represented an organizational shift toward innovation, adaptability, and precision—all elements that were critical to the Defense Mapping Agency's mission. This revolution in cartography was a demonstration of what could be accomplished with vision, dedication, and a relentless focus on meeting the needs of those who rely on us to achieve their missions safely and effectively.

After contributing to the development of the Digital Production System, the next challenge was to begin to integrate its elements into actual production. I took on the assignment to return to St. Louis to make this happen. This transformation marked a significant milestone for the agency and held personal significance for me. Washington, DC, had served as my proving ground, where I had honed my skills as a program manager. This role required strategic thinking, foresight, and the ability to unite diverse teams under a common vision. Yet, despite the project's magnitude, I knew the true challenge awaited me in St. Louis.

The shift from manual mapmaking, with its colored pencils and physical materials, to a fully digital workflow embodied progress. But progress came with challenges. With implementation on the horizon, I had to transition myself, too, from managing contracts to managing people. Pay disputes, performance reviews, and even the rare, somber duty of issuing pink slips became part of my new reality. The work expanded beyond innovation, focusing instead on managing the human element of change management.

CHAPTER 5

LEADERSHIP IN THE MAKING

"The world breaks everyone and afterward many are strong at the broken places."

—ERNEST HEMINGWAY

My leap from technical expert to general manager was a trial by fire. The weight of change tested me as I overhauled workflows, addressed team anxieties, and felt the human cost of progress. This chapter explores how these "broken places" built a more empathetic leadership style, proving that even amid profound change, growth and resilience could prevail.

When	1986	1987	1988	1989
Rank	GS-15			
Location	DMAAC (St. Louis)			

FROM WASHINGTON TO ST. LOUIS

Stepping away from Washington, DC, after four years was bittersweet. I felt both a sense of accomplishment and a pang of hesitation. My time in the nation's capital had been nothing short of transformative. There I sharpened my skills as a program manager, pushing technological boundaries and turning raw data into actionable innovation. This massive program was about strategy, aligning government and contractor teams with diverse backgrounds, priorities, and skillsets around a unified vision. Washington tested me in ways I could have never anticipated.

The modernization program was a monumental one, a precursor to something far larger on the horizon. Yet, as critical as that work was, I knew the real challenge awaited me back in St. Louis, at the Defense Mapping Agency Aerospace Center where I had started my career years earlier as a fresh-faced GS-5 mathematician. But this time, I wasn't coming back as the same person. I was returning to jump-start an organizational transition that would take years of tradition and, quite literally, redraw it into a new reality.

BACK TO BUILDING 36

The Arsenal's Building 36 held my entire St. Louis DMA career, from starting as a GS-5 mathematician, advancing to GS-12 cartographer, and now as GS-15 Chief of the Production Programs Modernization Division. Returning to help begin the transition into digital map production, I carried fresh insights from the Exploitation Modernization Program, but I faced a hesitant team deeply rooted in DMAAC's traditional workflows. The parallels were undeniable. Just as Building 36's facade seemed to resist the march of time, many of the people and traditions inside resisted the digital wave about to sweep through the agency. This wasn't simple stubbornness; it was the tension that comes from pride in one's craft being threatened by unfamiliar tools.

My office, tucked inside this architecturally significant building, was modest, a different story from the mere desk I'd occupied when I first started here. This was a space defined by purpose. At its core was the conference table that abutted my desk, its surface perpetually layered with marked-up reports, technical diagrams, and binders full of data on the digital production systems. The absence of windows, dictated by security protocols, left the space draped in a grim stillness.

THE DIGITAL TIDE

The cartographic world I had entered back in the mid-1970s was a tactile one. Maps were handcrafted with colored pencils, ink, stencils, and precision tools. Every line, every contour, every piece of data had an aesthetic human touch. But the future envisioned for DMA was vastly different. By the time I returned to St. Louis in 1986, digital mapmaking had evolved into a clear mandate rather than just a distant concept. We were tasked with building the plan to replace manual methods with digitally assisted workflows, ushering in an era where computers, rather than people with rulers and protractors, would interpret terrain and produce maps. For geospatial intelligence, this shift would become the backbone of a modernized defense infrastructure.

But progress wasn't linear, and while digital tools promised precision and efficiency, they came wrapped in challenges that were neither digital nor at all precise. Turning a vision into reality required effort on every level, reshaping not only workflows but also the lives of individuals who had dedicated years to mastering crafts now on the brink of obsolescence. This was more than replacing technology; it was about replacing mindsets.

NAVIGATING THE LABYRINTH

Stepping into this world of organizational change management was like entering a labyrinth, a completely new and different challenge than any I'd faced before. Suddenly, I was thrust into a world where progress was measured in millimeters, not miles. Every decision, every minor adjustment, had to be justified with mountains of paperwork and endless meetings—like navigating a complex maze with invisible walls and shifting pathways.

Bureaucratic processes, once viewed as necessary evils from afar, now loomed over every task. The sheer inertia of the system was overwhelming, like trying to steer a massive ship with a rusty rudder. Even the smallest course correction required immense effort and patience.

This immersion in bureaucracy revealed a stark truth: Human systems, even in the face of technological revolution, can be incredibly resistant to change. People clung to familiar processes, fearing the unknown, and the organization itself seemed to resist any deviation from the established way of doing things. This constant resistance served as a reminder that progress involves more than just implementing new technologies; true advancement requires overcoming deeply ingrained habits and structures that keep organizations from moving forward.

I quickly learned that altering how people worked proved far more challenging than modifying software. The process demanded a deeper appreciation for their anxieties, resistance, and emotional ties to familiar practices. My role demanded empathy, patience, and a whole new set of leadership skills I had to develop on the fly.

WHISPERS OF CHANGE

But beneath the surface of this structured world, whispers circulated. This wind of change wove watercooler whispers of woe, as rumors of a possible RIF (reduction in force) cast a shadow over many conversations. The uncertainty hung in the air like an unspoken question, leaving people on edge and awaiting answers.

The onset of digital processes—computer mice replacing pencils and digital imagery replacing film photographs—threatened much more than tradition. Our task was to lay the groundwork for a transition to digital map production, an urgent necessity that would reshape how we worked. Since my planning team was not directly involved in the production workflow, we faced a lower risk of layoffs. However, the transition plan we were crafting could result in job losses for others, including friends and even family members.

The weight of that reality was crushing. Every decision came with an unspoken question: Whose livelihood would this cost? Helping to lead this transformation was no small task, and as chief of the Division, I often felt the enormity of that weight.

BRIDGING THE GAP

I'd seen the future in the Exploitation Modernization Program. Digital production systems meant a sea change, but this vision felt like a foreign language to many on my team. I struggled to translate it into something relatable. "We're adapting as we go," one analyst told me, and it stung because it rang true. This was my mistake. For a while, I had been delegating assignments without providing clarity about the "why."

This organizational upheaval required more than tools like resource management; it demanded honesty, patience, and vulnerability. Slowly, those green walls bore witness to guarded trust evolving into collaboration. Together, we faced the uncertainty, moving toward a shared and uncharted future.

MANAGING PEOPLE

For me personally, the transition was just as profound. The DC years had been centered around managing contracts and collaborating with external organizations, but back in St. Louis, my focus shifted to managing people. It was, frankly, a paradigm shift I hadn't fully anticipated. At times, I wondered if my knack for organizing technical systems and timelines could translate to addressing the human element in all its complexity.

Personnel performance reviews were one of my first wake-up calls. Quantifying someone's contributions by fitting them into an HR-issued bell curve was never easy, especially when the work was as nuanced as production plans and policy. These reviews backed us into tough conversations about performance, attitude, and sometimes even aptitude for a new, digital reality. While some employees absorbed feedback with grace, others pushed back, their sense of self-worth bruised. My job, I realized, was to mentor, guide, and, where necessary, extend a hand to those who needed and wanted help adapting.

Then there were the annual performance bonus pool disputes—an inherently charged process. When someone's bonus didn't align with their expectations, or worse, their self-worth, it was a deeply personal one, and the ripple effects extended through teams, shaking morale.

I initially thought I could mitigate these negative reactions by sacrificing my own bonus to create a larger overall fund, which would then allow for more generous bonuses for my team. It turned out they barely noticed the increase, and I received no recognition or appreciation for having done it. I quickly learned that addressing these disputes was more about listening, showing empathy, and being firm than it was about money.

The most somber duty, however, was witnessing the issuing of pink slips. They were to be issued to individuals whose positions were being rendered obsolete as the organization moved forward, transitioning into an era of updated processes and advanced technology. For those affected, the modernization represented a profound and deeply personal upheaval.

Though I wasn't the one delivering the pink slips, I watched as a whiteboard in a nearby office became a battlefield map, marking the precise locations of desks now marked by the ominous arrival of white envelopes, each concealing a pink slip inside. The trail of envelopes grew, weaving through the map of the building drawn on that board—an eerie choreography, rigid and unrelenting.

The weight of my role in shaping the future production plans felt inescapable. My efforts in the modernization program had contributed to sketching the blueprint for change, outlining roles that would eventually become obsolete. This step was essential for progress but came with a deeply human cost. Years earlier, when I first encountered the hulking IBM 1620, I sensed the inevitable rise of automation and its potential to reshape the DMA workforce. Now, witnessing the tangible consequences of that shift, the pink slips, the displaced employees, the human cost of progress, was sobering. The experience served as a stark reminder that innovation, while necessary, comes with a price.

What haunted me most in these moments was how impersonal progress could feel. Here we were, advancing technology for the betterment of national defense, streamlining data, and leaping into the digital age, yet the cost of conversion was painfully tangible. The toll was evident in livelihoods lost, strained relationships, and the investment of both time and money.

Still, for all the trials, St. Louis offered me its own opportunities to grow, both for DMAAC as an institution and for me as a leader. I developed a deeper understanding of what leadership and management required. I was not only expected to manage resources and production quotas but also cultivate an environment where team members felt heard and valued, even amid sweeping change.

Looking back, the years of facilitating DMAAC's transition from manual to digital were about navigating both technological advancements and the human dynamics they impacted. Even when the days felt overwhelming, I returned home each night with a strong sense of responsibility for the people creating the maps, recognizing that progress would mean changing the way we worked and empowered those doing the work.

THE MEMO THAT CHANGED EVERYTHING

By February 1989, I felt like I had finally hit my stride as a GS-15 supervisor. For the first time in my career, everything seemed to align. Our efforts to plan the integration of the new digital mapmaking equipment were reaching fruition, and I'd carved out meaningful progress in aligning my team with the transition mission in front of us. We were preparing to modernize what once seemed an archaic process, and witnessing the early results of that conversion filled me with pride.

Everything seemed headed in the right direction. Then that feeling of stability shattered with a single memo. It was a directive, cold and official, informing me I was being reassigned back to Washington, DC. The decision was unexpected and devastating. Any hope I had for a sense of permanence evaporated.

A NEW ROLE, A HEAVY BURDEN

Professionally, I was to become the assistant deputy director of the modernization group. The title sounded grand, but the reality was far more burdensome than prestigious. I'd been assigned to lead a DMA center activation team, a joint government-contractor venture responsible for bringing the new digital production system online and into full production across various centers. The job's scope was enormous. This included approving schedule and technical changes, ensuring readiness through rehearsals and training exercises, and designing initial production loads for the centers based on DMA guidance.

I was to manage a team of senior professionals, most at my own GS-15 rank. Engineers, specialists, and contractors filled the team, their work intersecting under my direction. With so many responsibilities in play, it felt like sitting on a knife's edge. I had to balance the technical precision of the DPS system with strict deadlines, all while operating in Washington, DC—far from home.

UPROOTED AGAIN

Despite my professional resolve, the personal impact was harder to weather. My family had barely unpacked in St. Louis when we were told to uproot once again. My wife and children had settled into our new house, and now they were being forced to leave all of it behind at a moment's notice. There were no guarantees in Washington. No serene neighborhood waiting for us, no schools woven into the community fabric like the ones where my kids had thrived. For all that I had accomplished in St. Louis, what did I have to show for it? A reassignment and the daunting prospect of starting over, both at work and at home.

Committed to my responsibilities, I packed my bags and

headed off alone to prepare for the move. I rented a small room temporarily and spent my days at work, while my nights were split between house hunting and grappling with the emotions of this transition. On paper, I fulfilled my duties—overseeing rehearsals, approving technical changes, and coordinating with a talented team of colleagues and contractors. Yet, beneath the surface, I struggled to reconcile the sacrifices of home life with the demands of my career. I was not unhappy with DMA; in fact, I respected the mission I was a part of. But I couldn't ignore the internal tug-of-war between my desire to contribute to something bigger than myself and the simple longing for stability for my family.

Each day felt like a balancing act as I worked to meet professional expectations while carrying a quiet hope of finding a path that wouldn't force me to choose between serving the mission and preserving the life I had built in St. Louis. Meetings felt hollow, and milestones seemed overshadowed by the knowledge that I was far from where I wanted to be geographically and in my sense of fulfillment. The excitement and purpose I once felt in St. Louis seemed to dissipate with each passing day, replaced by a growing sense of displacement. While I valued the opportunities and challenges of my new role, I couldn't shake the longing for comfort and connection. The constant uncertainty weighed heavily on me, leaving me yearning for a way to harmonize contribution with the life I had worked so hard to build.

FATE IN THE CHECKOUT AISLE

It was meant to be a quick trip home, a brief reprieve from the demands of work. Over Easter, I found myself back in the comforting familiarity of my home near St. Louis, reconnecting with family and savoring a sense of belonging. Little did I know this visit would set the stage for one of the most pivotal moments of my life.

Like any good local, I made the obligatory stop at the supermarket for last-minute supplies. While debating whether I needed a hollow chocolate bunny or a solid one, something caught my eye—the freebie Scott AFB newspaper sitting by the checkout counter. Out of curiosity, I picked it up. And there it was, an article about the newly established United States Transportation Command (USTRANSCOM). Officially established two years earlier, it was growing in inertia and recruiting civilians for critical positions. My pulse quickened. Fate, it seemed, was dangling an opportunity right before me.

A BOLD MOVE

On a whim and a prayer, I contacted the personnel office at Scott, the very place where my civil service career had started many years earlier. I couldn't believe my luck. They had a GS-15 vacancy in the IT department of USTRANSCOM, which perfectly aligned with my qualifications. There was a caveat: The position would typically go through a lengthy competitive recruitment process. But an interagency transfer could circumvent the red tape entirely *if* I could convince the hiring manager to support the transfer. This was my chance to stay close to home and broaden my career by joining a new, important, and growing organization.

It was a gamble, and I knew it. When I arrived for my meeting with the hiring official, an imposing Army Colonel, the stakes couldn't have been higher. A Vietnam veteran with a southern drawl as rough as gravel, his commanding presence filled the room. His no-nonsense demeanor and open disdain for bureaucracy were impossible to miss. He barely tolerated the "climate controlled" Air Force culture, had zero regard for the complexities of the civilian hiring process, and even less tolerance for its delays.

While I respected his hard edge, I also saw my opening. This was someone who valued action over red tape, efficiency over process. Winning him over would be no small feat, but I had a plan.

I laid my cards on the table. "You have a choice," I told him candidly. "You can wait for the lengthy and cumbersome Air Force recruitment process to run its course, which I would be happy to explain to you—in detail—and then risk getting stuck with someone you don't want. *Orrrr* you can act now. Your signature on the form I am holding in my hand will immediately initiate my lateral transfer from DMA into your vacant position—no red tape, no waiting, no paperwork purgatory. I'm already a GS-15 with the exact knowledge, skills, and experience you need in that position and I would be honored to work for you."

The Colonel eyed me with a mix of suspicion and wariness, the look of someone who had heard one too many pitches starting with, "I'm from Washington and I'm here to help." Still, I had his attention. He was open to the idea but clearly struggling to believe that dealing with bureaucracy could ever be anything but a slow-motion train wreck. I could almost see the gears in his head protesting, "Can it be that easy?" Regardless, he likely figured he had little to lose and everything to gain. Plus, getting to take a free shot at the Air Force bureaucracy would be icing on the cake.

With a firm handshake, the deal was sealed. Just like that, my future shifted. I stepped into a role that would shape my career in profound ways. Just like that, I was headed to a fresh start at USTRANSCOM.

HOMECOMING

Joining USTRANSCOM was a homecoming of sorts. When I first arrived at Scott Air Force Base as a GS-1 clerk fifteen years earlier, I never could have imagined the path my career would take. Yet here I was, about to return, not as a low-level clerk but as Technical Director for the IT organization under the newly formed United States Transportation Command.

This was more than just a job. The role represented the culmination of years of learning, growth, and perseverance, and it set the stage for my eventual promotion to the Senior Executive Service in the Pentagon.

That serendipitous moment in the supermarket, a chance encounter with a newspaper, remains burned in my memory. Sometimes, the most defining opportunities are the ones we least expect, and the boldest moves can lead to the most extraordinary outcomes.

PART III

USTRANSCOM

DESERT SHIELD AND BEYOND

Step back into the 1980s with me, a time of floppy disks and dial-up modems, as I embarked on a new chapter at Scott Air Force Base with the US Transportation Command. Hungry to contribute to missions of national significance, I navigated the new complexities of a joint military command, played a role in pivotal operations like Desert Shield and Desert Storm, and pursued leadership within the Senior Executive Service. This move was also a homecoming, bringing the comfort of a familiar community amid the intensity of a new role.

Shifting from optimizing production processes at DMA to managing the technical demands of a military command was a challenge. At USTRANSCOM, the consequences of mistakes could affect national defense and human lives, demanding urgency, adaptability, and resilience. Amid the pressure, there were moments of camaraderie, like dodgeball games with Generals, and moments of trial, like system crashes that forced us to innovate on the fly. These experiences stretched my perspective and shaped my leadership approach.

Part III is a story of transformation and growth, capturing the significance of finding my footing in high-stakes environments.

CHAPTER 6

DIGITAL HIGHWAYS

NAVIGATING IT CHALLENGES AND INNOVATIONS

"Bill, you need to learn the difference between RPM and MPH."
—MY ARMY COLONEL SUPERVISOR AT USTRANSCOM

This lesson in leadership, delivered with a classic Army BLUF (Bottom Line Up Front) style, emphasized the importance of focusing on outcomes over activity. It's a reminder that true progress (miles per hour versus revolutions per minute) comes from taking action and achieving measurable outcomes.

When	1989	1990
Rank	GS-15	
Location	USTRANSCOM (Scott AFB)	

BUILDING 1961

April 1989. Driving toward the edge of Scott Air Force Base, a wave of familiarity swept over me. The open fields surrounding Scott had been the backdrop of my childhood, where the drone of aircraft overhead was as constant as the Midwest wind. Scott AFB was the heartbeat of the county, where dreams could take flight even if the runways weren't yours to walk.

Now, fifteen years later, I was returning, not for just another job, but for a homecoming. My civil service career had started nearby as a GS-1, a rookie learning the ropes and savoring the pride of a tiny civil service paycheck. But this time, I was stepping into a pivotal new role as Technical Director of the IT arm of US Transportation Command (USTRANSCOM). A lot had changed, yet Scott still felt like unfinished business, a story waiting for its next chapter.

Pulling into the parking lot of Building 1961, memories hit me with a force I couldn't ignore. The building's plain metal exterior stood as it always had, unremarkable and unassuming, as if forgotten by time. The railroad tracks nearby still stretched along the fence line, dividing the base from the surrounding farm fields, where familiar family-run businesses carried on, untouched by the years. Though the setting was much the same, I was not. The wide-eyed clerk I'd once been had grown into a leader, returning now to build on a career shaped by persistence and purpose.

Building 1961 itself carried its own layered story. The structure had once served as the base commissary before being repurposed into office space. Local lore whispered rumors that it had even been condemned at one point. Now, it sat on the outskirts of Scott's bustling operations, a far cry from the other buildings where most of the command action unfolded. It wasn't much to look at, but it was ours, essential and enduring, even in its isolation.

As I walked inside, the cool air brought with it the distinct smell of industrial cleaner mingled with an earthy, metallic undertone—a nod to the building's history. The long hallway ahead stretched like a tunnel, its plain industrial carpeting muffling my footsteps. Overhead, bundles of cables were threaded through the ceiling, regularly peeking out through a few missing panels, a quiet declaration of the building's role in keeping things running behind the scenes.

And then there were the orange traffic cones. A cluster of them surrounded a damp, dark spot on the hallway carpet, evidence of a roof that leaked persistently, refusing to be fully repaired. These cones, their bright plastic incongruously cheerful in the drabness, became an indelible image for me. They symbolized the resilience of this building and, by extension, the work we did here in IT. We were the silent systems that supported USTRANSCOM's operational might, essential but often removed from the spotlight.

THE IT TEAM

Our team's mission was simple but indispensable. We were the ones who ensured computers stayed functional, networks remained connected, and phones worked seamlessly. While higher-profile teams carried out the more visible operations, our division operated like those exposed cables overhead—quiet, integral, and often taken for granted.

Yet, the people brought Building 1961 to life in a way its architecture never could. Warm smiles and professional nods from colleagues were constants in its hallways, their shared purpose creating an atmosphere of determination. Inside shared workspaces, muted conversations and occasional laughter cut through the building's starkness, filling the space with humanity and collaboration.

That leaky roof. Those snaking cables. The faintly buzzing lights and the musty scent. They were markers of something much bigger. Beyond the quirks and imperfections of Building 1961 lay a place that embodied resilience and purpose. Here my professional road came full circle, where every moment of my career up to now coalesced into something greater.

CROSSING INTO UNITY

This was USTRANSCOM, a joint military command like nothing I had ever encountered. Walking through its offices was like stepping into a living mosaic, alive with the vibrant blend of service cultures, uniforms, and insignias—Air Force blues mingling with Army greens, Navy whites, Marine khakis, and Coast Guard blues. This mix of military services is why it was called a joint command—a tangible tapestry of military camaraderie, woven together with purpose and pride, and it was exhilarating to witness this harmony on what was culturally an Air Force stronghold.

I saw how perspectives from different military branches and civilian experts, government employees and contractors from contrasting organizational cultures, came together to tackle complex problems. USTRANSCOM's joint military environment was a dynamic crucible of strategies, expertise, and approaches. The journey wasn't always smooth, but the results were remarkable. We all understood the gravity of our mission and the need to accomplish it. Creativity born from diverse perspectives ensured that we explored every reasonable idea in pursuit of mission accomplishment because we knew we were responsible and would be held accountable for delivering against that mission.

DIVERSITY OF THOUGHT

Whether it was an Air Force pilot proposing an unconventional programming approach or a Navy submariner rethinking operational challenges, ideas were judged by their merit and practicality, not the rank or role of the speaker. When diverse perspectives were guided by a shared sense of responsibility, filtered through a lens of merit, and reinforced by a "best idea wins" mentality, the potential for progress was unlimited.

The sheer diversity of thought and experience sparked an infectious energy that buzzed through the offices. It was a creative symphony where each branch brought its unique rhythm to the mix. Solutions leaped out of the interplay of these varied perspectives—ideas that likely wouldn't have emerged if each service had worked in isolated teams. You could see this spirited unity in the friendly rivalries that played out, from boisterous debates over who was the best at what, to cheeky banter like "Go Army, Beat Navy!" These moments weren't just amusing; they were the glue that strengthened bonds and deepened respect. The culture of collaboration was functional and foundational. Competition here wasn't divisive; it was a bonding agent.

A NEW KIND OF OPERATION

This was my initiation into a world I hadn't even begun to comprehend—a place where operations happened on a scale and intensity I couldn't have imagined while cocooned in software obscurity of the Defense Mapping Agency. Back at DMA, I had been in my own corner of the world, a mental one, filled with the intricacies of mathematics and code, aware of but removed from the pulse of active military life. But here? I had entered an entirely new game with different players, new rules, and high stakes.

I'll admit it: Before stepping into USTRANSCOM, I didn't know a sink from a CINC (Commander in Chief), and new acronyms zoomed past me faster than jets. This was a different universe. For the first time, I saw the intricate choreography of military branches working together, and I felt like I'd been thrown into a fast-moving current in which I had no choice but to swim. To navigate this new world, I had to quickly learn the language and structure of a joint military command, including the "J" directorates: J1 for Human Resources, J2 for Intelligence, J3 for Operations, J4 for Logistics, J5 for Strategy, and J6 for my own IT organization. Each directorate played a crucial role in the command's mission, and understanding their functions and interdependencies was essential for effective teamwork and leadership.

MY WORKSPACE

In my tiny, personal command center, the organization's energy transformed into a one-on-one battle with dot matrix printers, floppy disks, and the temperamental hum of a dial-up modem. The shift was striking, yet in this cluttered workspace, complete with its symphony of clicks, whirs, and beeps, I found the same sense of purpose. Just as military branches worked in harmony, I began to piece together my own rhythm amid the chaos.

I dove into setting up my cubicle, transforming the neutral tones of my workspace into my beige fortress of productivity. The fabric-lined walls stood proud, encircling my desk, which was dominated by a hulking desktop PC. With its mighty 256K of memory, it sat like the crown jewel of my small kingdom. Occasionally, the *tap-tap-tap* of a typewriter would filter through, but word processing was the new frontier. WordStar, my trusty friend, battled valiantly against the clunky, user-hostile Microsoft Word for dominance. To this day, I wish I still had WordStar. Now that was a program with character. With its raw display of formatting codes, it was like a classic car engine, no frills or hidden electronics, just the raw mechanics of formatting laid bare for me to tinker with and understand.

Under the desk lurked my dot matrix printer, a noisy, essential monster that would leap into action with a tinny mechanical buzz—*zzzzzzzzzzt, zzzzzzzzzzt*—spitting out documents with gusto. Printouts would pile up in perforated strips, creating a happy mess of papers with neatly torn edges scattered all around. The scene was complete chaos but, oddly enough, felt indispensable, like an orchestra tuning up before the show.

Floppy disks—5.25 inches of retro chaos—were a ubiquitous and temperamental presence. They were everywhere: scattered across my desk, stuffed into desk drawers, and tucked into thin, tattered cardboard boxes. Each disk carried a thrilling gamble of hope and anxiety. Kilobytes (not megabytes or gigabytes) of fragile data spun in their little plastic hearts, until a mischievous gremlin, armed with static electricity, would swoop in, and *poof!* That precious cargo was corrupted faster than you could say "disk error." Floppies were the divas of data storage, full of potential but with a flair for catastrophe. I labeled each one meticulously, relying on my trusty permanent marker whose sharp scent clung to the air, mingling with the faint but constant aroma of warm electronics and aging office furniture.

My workspace was a feast for the nose and memorably loud. The internet as we know it was still more of an idea than a reality. Instead, communication came via heavy manuals, endless paper memos, and the occasional screech of a fax machine. My dial-up modem was its own unwelcome performer, launching into a scratchy, high-pitched song every time I tried to connect to the digital world.

This office, messy, noisy, smelly, colorless, and wonderfully alive, was a sensory symphony. Somewhere between the floppy disks, fabric walls, and screeching modems, I found more than an everyday job. This was the start of something extraordinary, and every funny, frustrating, and gratifying moment of it solidified my love for this chapter of my career.

LESSONS IN ACTION: FROM RPM TO MPH

My first supervisor at USTRANSCOM was the Army Colonel whom I had met earlier while negotiating my transfer from DMA to USTRANSCOM. Assigned to J6, he was one of the many non–Air Force military personnel that enriched the command's diversity. His communication style was classic Army BLUF: straight to the point and delivered with precision that could rival a sniper's rifle. But just when you thought he couldn't be more intense, he'd drop a joke or a perfectly timed one-liner that caught you off guard and left you chuckling. His humor was disarming, the kind of wit that made you feel like you were part of his team, no matter how high the stakes. His "take that hill" attitude, rooted in muddy boots and frontline determination, set him apart in a space dominated by the clean precision and formality of Air Force culture.

The occasional curl of cigarette smoke coming from his office desk drawer symbolized something larger than nicotine. Despite the rules in that strict nonsmoking facility, he would occasionally light one up, not flagrantly, but just enough to signal something larger. The act was more than just habit. The gesture was his quiet rebellion, a subtle reminder to everyone around him that he was *Army*, through and through. That small defiance encapsulated his essence—independent and unconcerned about bending to Air Force bureaucratic formalities when they didn't serve the mission.

What made him especially memorable was his thoughtful and instructive nature. He had a way of imparting lessons that stuck, boiling complicated principles down into simple truths.

"Bill," he once told me, an unlit cigarette hanging loosely from his lips, "you need to learn the difference between RPM and MPH. Noise ain't progress; motion is. Give me a progress report, not a status report." This was his sharp reminder to focus on results, not activity. He valued action over appearances, results over posturing.

As I stood under the flicker of fluorescent lights in that utilitarian building, I knew I'd carry this lesson well beyond those walls. RPM and MPH weren't just numbers. They were a mantra for how to set expectations and make progress in any challenge ahead.

My supervisor's emphasis on action and results resonated throughout USTRANSCOM, shaping not only our work ethic but also our approach to team building. This focus on "motion over noise" even extended to our after-hours activities, and one particular event stands out as a prime example: a dodgeball game that brought out the competitive spirit in everyone, including an unexpected participant.

HIGH-STAKES DODGEBALL

At USTRANSCOM back in the '90s, team-building events were as unpredictable as they were entertaining. Every month, one of our J6 offices had the honor (or curse) of planning an activity, something to help us bond, unwind, and ideally not cause any permanent injuries. Previous events had their own infamous legacies, like the chili cook-off where someone's "secret spicy ingredient" required a fire extinguisher for a tongue, or the square-dancing class that proved most of us should never, ever attempt the do-si-do.

These events typically happened in the early evening, after hours, when the only thing louder than our jokes was the laughter and the creak of worn office chairs. But this time, our office decided to up the stakes. Someone suggested dodgeball, and we were all in.

The large conference room became our war zone. Tables and chairs were pushed aside, and the participants assembled. Fat, squishy playground balls in hand, we kicked off an evening of laughter, friendly rivalry, and surprising athleticism. The LAN (local area network) admins zipped around like caffeinated ninjas, sys admins (system administrators) calculated their tosses like they were debugging an impossible code error, secretaries dodged with an elegance that only years of dodging deadlines could bring, and the mainframe crew? Silent assassins. Their throws came out of nowhere like they'd been plotting revenge for decades in those quiet server rooms.

The game was chaotic perfection until the conference room doors suddenly swung open. And there he was, the Commander of USTRANSCOM himself. A four-star General. A fighter and airlift pilot with a reputation that spanned Presidents and continents.

Everything froze. Someone dropped a ball, and it rolled solemnly across the floor. For a second, we thought we were about to get our orders pulled due to "improper workplace conduct."

But then he smiled. The tension broke, and we all exhaled, but before anyone could explain away the makeshift dodgeball court, he did the unthinkable. He bent down, grabbed one of the balls, and said, "Who needs reinforcements?" A ripple of excitement went through the room as he joined the opposing team.

It was as surreal as it was intimidating, and I...I saw my opportunity.

I sized him up. Sure, he was a legend. A strategic and tactical Air Force genius. But this was dodgeball, not an F-15. I figured, "He might own the skies, but here on the carpeted battlefield of our large conference room? He's just another player." If I could take him out with a well-placed shot, I'd have bragging rights for the rest of my career.

I thought I had the upper hand. After all, I had thirty-ish youth, decent reflexes, and questionable judgment on my side. But, as it turned out, none of that mattered.

I hung back, crouching behind a teammate. I had him locked in on my mental radar. Circling, I waited for the right moment to throw the ball. Then, quick as a wink, I jumped out and fired my 250mm rubber cannon. And MISSED! The ball floated past him so slowly it could have been a weather balloon.

He didn't hesitate. With fighter pilot instincts, he locked eyes on me. His grin was half respect, half predatory. He mouthed *Fox 1!*—Air Force jargon for releasing a missile—and launched his counterattack. The ball sailed toward me with the precision and speed of a Sidewinder missile. I tried to dodge with all the grace of a breakdancing giraffe, jumping and twisting midair in what I can only describe as "chaotic flail mode." None of it mattered. Direct hit. Right to the stomach.

Without missing a beat, the General gave me a quick look, as if to say, "Nice try, kid," then turned his attention to other targets as I shamefully stumbled off to the "out" zone, ego bruised but spirit intact.

That night was unforgettable, cementing itself as the crown jewel in my J6 entertainment memories. For years afterward, every time I saw him, whether in person or on TV, I could practically hear him say, *Check six, kid*—an aviator's reminder to stay aware of your surroundings and be ready to face the unexpected whether in a dogfight or a conference room.

Lesson learned, Sir. Lesson learned.

The dodgeball game was more than just a fun diversion; it was a microcosm of camaraderie, adaptability, and quick thinking that defined our work at USTRANSCOM. Just as we navigated the unexpected on the makeshift court, we faced real-world challenges that demanded innovative solutions and collaborative effort. One such challenge was addressing the gap in civilian training—a critical issue that required the same spirit of teamwork and ingenuity.

A CRYSTAL BALL

Let's be honest—most people found civilian training to be a dull topic. Leaders knew how to wage wars, but training the civilian workforce? That was murky territory, a back-burner issue that rarely commanded serious attention.

But to me, civilian training was an elephant in the room—a clear gap in organizational effectiveness that no one wanted to confront. Year after year, it suffered from weak justifications and half-hearted interest, dismissed as little more than bureaucratic noise. Yet I saw the cracks that formed in real time. Vacancies sat unfilled, morale slumped, and important training initiatives struggled to secure even the most basic funding. The cost of neglect was right in front of me, but the conversation was stuck in neutral.

So, I created a tool called the Civilian Training Requirements System (CTRS) to take this overlooked, undervalued issue and place it firmly in the spotlight. CTRS was a crystal ball of sorts, forecasting the training required to keep our civilian workforce ready for their roles. By extracting information from the Command's personnel system, the system analyzed the records of our civilian workforce and calculated an inventory in work years of specific skills (for example, project management) at each grade level. I programmed it to factor in attrition rates and projected vacancies, then estimate the amount of those skills we'd need in the future. The gap between the skills we had and the skills we would need drove the training requirement and budget request. This data-driven approach painted a clear picture for decision-makers, mapping out skills gaps, attrition patterns, and training investments using the Command's own data without wishing, whining, or whimsy.

The system's objectivity and scalability were its greatest strengths: Not only did it serve as a powerful tool for the civilians in our Command, but it also could be scaled up and applied across the entire Air Force's civilian computer and communications career development program.

CTRS spoke a language decision-makers understood—the language of data, impact, and return on investment. The program demonstrated that training was a necessary investment in workforce readiness and mission success. And in the process, it painted a clear picture of my own capabilities, my strategic vision, and my drive to deliver impactful results.

The development of CTRS was a pivotal achievement, capturing the attention of Air Force leadership and showcasing my ability to drive enterprise-wide, mission-focused solutions.

Little did I know that these early days at USTRANSCOM were just the prelude to a period of intense challenges, unexpected crises, and remarkable displays of teamwork and innovation.

CHAPTER 7

TRIAL BY FIRE

SAVING THE SYSTEM, SAVING THE MISSION

"It doesn't take a hero to order men into battle. It takes a hero to be one of those men who goes into battle."

—GENERAL H. NORMAN SCHWARZKOPF

This quote resonates with the challenges and triumphs of Chapter 7, where I wasn't on the front lines but played a crucial role in supporting those who were. When the WWMCCS/JOPES (Worldwide Military Command and Control System/Joint Operational Planning and Execution System) crashed during Operation Desert Storm, it was my team and I who worked tirelessly to restore critical communication and logistics capabilities. This quote serves as a reminder of the courage and dedication of those who serve in the military, and the importance of those of us who support them behind the scenes.

When	1990	1991	1992	1993	1994	1995
Rank	GS-15					SES
Location	USTRANSCOM (Scott AFB)					Pentagon

THE WWMCCS/JOPES SYSTEM

The steady hum of computers filled the air as a constant reminder of the crucial connection between technology and global security. At USTRANSCOM's nerve center, these state-of-the-art systems managed the complex choreography of troops, supplies, and equipment moving across the globe. Then one day, that steady rhythm was abruptly interrupted by an urgent alarm. The WWMCCS/JOPES system, the backbone of our military's logistical planning, had crashed. The stakes were enormous. This outage threatened to disrupt operations on a worldwide scale. Leading a team of developers, I was tasked with ensuring the system's recovery and safeguarding its reliability in the face of such a critical failure.

This moment made it clear just how vital these systems were to our mission. To understand the gravity of the situation, it's important to grasp the groundbreaking role of the Worldwide Military Command and Control System (WWMCCS, pronounced "wim-ix") and a core application, the Joint Operational Planning and Execution System (JOPES).

Emerging in the 1980s, WWMCCS was a distributed network of computers that transformed military command, control, and communications. These computers were interconnected and constantly synchronized with each other, so that if one of them crashed or perhaps was destroyed during a war, the others would continue to run and support the military operation without missing a beat. Designed for real-time, global data sharing, WWMCCS provided enhanced situational awareness, enabling the precise coordination of large-scale troop movements and the delivery of critical equipment. A critical component of this network was JOPES, a software application that facilitated logistical and operational planning. Running on Honeywell mainframe computers, JOPES was indispensable to

USTRANSCOM's mission, generating the detailed plans that enabled forces and resources to reach their destinations with precision and efficiency.

COLLABORATION IS KEY

At the heart of this effort was my team in USTRANSCOM/J6. Comprising government civilians and contractors, we were responsible for maintaining and advancing JOPES. Our primary goal was to meet the needs of USTRANSCOM's combined J3 (Operations) and J4 (Logistics) teams, the system's main users. These teams relied on JOPES to plan and execute complex operations, but significant challenges underscored our work. These challenges stemmed from physical distance, organizational divides, and functional differences between IT developers and operational staff.

Our IT team operated from a building physically removed from the J3/J4 organization, creating challenges of geographical separation and communication. This physical gap made regular collaboration difficult, leaving us out of step with their immediate operational needs. Organizationally, our roles were distinct, and our technical focus often clashed with their operational priorities, leading to misaligned expectations. Functionally, the J3/J4 teams didn't always grasp the technical complexity of software development, while we, as developers in the J6 organization, lacked firsthand insight into the logistical and operational realities they navigated.

Recognizing the critical need to bridge these divides, I spearheaded a cultural shift to improve collaboration. Standard communication methods, like email and briefings, weren't enough to close these gaps. Instead, I invited members of J3/J4 to join us in the J6/IT building and work alongside our developers. This was unconventional at the time, but necessary. By physically immersing operational staff in the development process, we fostered real-time feedback and mutual understanding.

AGILE BEFORE AGILE

This collaboration transformed the way we worked. Developers could consult immediately with users as they designed and refined new features. For instance, while building a logistics planning module, the J3/J4 staff highlighted operational blind spots, testing features on the spot, and guiding adjustments. This iterative process not only saved time but also ensured the software met real-world requirements.

The results were profound. We delivered JOPES updates more frequently, with higher user satisfaction and acceptance. Users felt valued, their input shaping systems that had a tangible impact on their work. This practice foreshadowed principles now central to Agile methodology, like cross-functional engagement, iterative development, and close user involvement. Additionally, it underscored the importance of identifying stakeholder mission champions—users who could bridge the gap between IT and operations.

Ultimately, these efforts reinforced the vital connection between technology and operational success. By closing divides and making users a part of the process, we didn't just improve software; we improved the way military teams coordinated efforts on a global scale. The lessons in bridging organizational divides, fostering collaboration, and delivering innovative solutions under tight deadlines directly prepared us for the immense challenges that unfolded during Desert Shield and Desert Storm. As global tensions escalated and USTRANSCOM filled its pivotal role of global military logistics coordination, the strategic insights and technical advances we honed through WWMCCS were no longer just concepts; they became tools that would drive real-world missions. The transition from system enhancements to operational execution marked a turning point, where our efforts in refining military planning systems were tested on a historic scale. Desert Shield was the arena where everything we had learned and achieved came to life, pushing us to apply our expertise under unprecedented pressure.

DESERT SHIELD/DESERT STORM

Operations Desert Shield and Desert Storm were pivotal Gulf War campaigns that underscored the power of coalition forces in defending Kuwait, successfully liberating the country through a strategic blend of defense and offensive precision. These landmark operations not only altered the conflict's trajectory but also highlighted the exceptional logistical and technological advancements that defined modern military strategy.

The groundwork was laid with Operation Desert Shield, one of the largest logistical efforts in military history. From August 1990 to March 1991, USTRANSCOM and its Army, Navy, and Air Force components facilitated the transport of 504,000 personnel, 3.6 million tons of cargo, and 6.1 million tons of fuel to the Persian Gulf.

Supported by USTRANSCOM's Crisis Action Team (CAT) and Joint Operations Center (JOC), these efforts showcased seamless coordination and execution on an unprecedented scale.

Historical comparisons amplify the magnitude of these achievements. More troops and equipment were moved in three weeks than during the first three months of the Korean War. Airlift operations surpassed the ton miles flown in the sixty-five-week Berlin Airlift within just six weeks, while sealift operations matched World War II's allied convoy volumes to Northern Russia in only five months.

TECHNOLOGY AT THE FOREFRONT

When Desert Storm launched, the integration of advanced technology and joint military forces became critical to success. I had the privilege of leading efforts to develop and release twenty-four major software updates for WWMCCS/JOPES over a remarkably short time frame. These updates enabled command centers to synchronize real-time data across military branches, ensuring commanders could make decisive, informed choices. This interoperability was indispensable to coordinating globally dispersed forces under extreme pressure, epitomizing modern technological precision.

What made this work extraordinary was its speed and impact during an era dominated by slow, mainframe-dependent processes. Despite immense challenges, our team delivered continuously tested software enhancements that supported operations and established a new benchmark for military software development. During this period, I embraced the mindset, "Stand on the rock of success, no matter how small," valuing incremental progress to deliver applications under pressure.

Ultimately, Desert Shield and Desert Storm set new standards for logistical coordination, technological innovation, and strategic execution in warfare. USTRANSCOM's achievements, coupled with software innovations, remain a testament to teamwork, adaptability, and precision—cornerstones of military success that still influence strategy today.

A SYSTEM IN CRISIS

During the intensity of Desert Storm, the WWMCCS/JOPES system, a vital tool for developing logistics and deployment plans, suffered a critical failure. The outage disrupted global synchronization across its databases, significantly hampering operations that relied on real-time data. US Transportation Command, still a young organization, faced mounting pressure as the disruption threatened to derail carefully coordinated efforts during a pivotal time for the mission.

Imagine a massive, intricate puzzle where every piece represents a soldier, a tank, a plane, or a supply truck needed for a mission. Now imagine that puzzle scattered across a map the size of the world. That's essentially what the WWMCCS/JOPES system was tracking during Desert Storm.

When the system crashed, it was like someone turned off the lights in the puzzle room. Suddenly, commanders couldn't see the whole picture through the lens of their computer screens. We wrestled with the magnitude of the outage. Talks grew grim, and doubts spread regarding the ability to restore the corrupted databases within the tight operational timeline.

INNOVATION UNDER PRESSURE

As Technical Director for USTRANSCOM's IT software division, I refused to believe the situation was beyond saving. While I didn't have an immediate solution, I knew that persistence and collective effort would uncover a path forward. I began reaching out to everyone, developers, engineers, and support staff, gathering ideas, no matter how unconventional. My goal was to spark creativity and mine the team's collective expertise for a breakthrough, one idea at a time.

Amid these conversations, I came across a young coder

whose creativity stood out despite his inexperience. I posed an open challenge to him: "If you could use any tool, any language, any method, what would you do?" The question was designed to remove limitations and foster bold thinking. Though initially unsure, he returned hours later with an unorthodox idea. His plan involved using his software language of choice to script a series of custom tools to reconstruct the corrupted databases and resynchronize them globally.

There were no guarantees, but the plan looked good. I gave him full support: resources, personnel, and trust to spearhead the endeavor. The team, energized yet anxious, worked tirelessly through the night. The atmosphere in the room buzzed with intensity as each person focused on their task while grappling with the weight of the mission. By dawn, the impossible had been achieved. The databases were restored, resynchronized, and fully operational. The disruption was resolved just in time to preserve the mission's trajectory. Then, to prevent further damage, we pinpointed the specific mainframe computer within the WWMCCS system that had been causing the issue and took it offline.

The relief in the room that morning was tangible. What could have been a catastrophic setback was transformed into a story of resilience, determination, and teamwork. Reflecting on the experience, I recognized critical lessons in leadership during a crisis. Persistence matters above all—unwavering determination to find solutions keeps the door open for possibilities. Leadership also means empowering individuals to think boldly and trusting their potential to contribute beyond expectations. Finally, collaboration is key. Every voice counts, and collective problem-solving can illuminate innovative paths forward when traditional methods fall short.

THE LOOSE FLOOR TILE

Even after resolving the immediate crisis, I couldn't rest until I unearthed the root cause of the corrupted databases and ensured it would never surface again.

The WWMCCS system's computers were woven together by a web of data pipes. Data moved through these pipes much like snail mail with computers packaging information into "envelopes" called packets, delivered by "mail carriers" known as digital communications processors.

To leave no stone unturned, I ordered an analysis of the data flowing into and out of the isolated data center's communications processor. Sitting at my desk, staring at streams of raw data, it felt like déjà vu. I was transported back to my early days of poring over data center hex dumps and deciphering DMA communication protocols bit by bit. Those experiences taught me patience and trained me to see patterns where others saw noise. That old instinct stirred now, sharper than I remembered.

After hours of scrutiny, I found it—tiny anomalies buried in the packets. Random characters slipped in where they didn't belong, like poison letters hidden in a bundle of mail. These corrupted packets looked normal enough to fool the system but wreaked havoc when processed, spreading errors to every connected database. Their sporadic nature made them maddeningly difficult to trace.

"Track every blip in the data streams," I instructed the team, urgency weighing in my voice. "Something has to be triggering this."

And then, a breakthrough. During one of the surges of corrupted packets, a message came from the data center—a technician had been in the room at the same moment the errors surfaced. Coincidence? It happened again. And again. Every time the system went haywire, an operator was nearby. The pattern was unmistakable.

Curiosity turned into urgency. I contacted the team at the data center and had them check everything from the hardware to the room's layout. That's when a hunch hit me. "Check the floor tiles," I said, almost on a whim. The randomness of the glitches struck something within me, reminding me of my mantra growing up: "Learn through your fingers." I've always believed in trying to tackle problems physically, getting to the core by touching the ground truth. Whether fixing a car or hammering a nail, engaging directly with the bones of the issue revealed insights no report or diagram ever could. That vivid, tactile approach had guided me before, and now, it was leading me toward the answer once again.

My hunch paid off. Beneath one particular tile, they found an exposed wire that sparked whenever someone stepped on that tile. The wire shifted *just enough* to cause electrical interference, injecting bad signals into the data flow, triggering a cascade of corrupted packets. That innocent step became the first domino, toppling everything in its path.

The problem was absurdly simple, yet devastatingly effective. A faulty cable underfoot transformed routine steps into tiny sparks of chaos. But now we had our answer. The repair was simple, and the system returned to order.

Standing in my cubicle at USTRANSCOM, I thought about how close we'd come to missing it entirely, and how those old skills, honed years ago with hex dumps and communications protocols, had guided me to the solution. Solving the mystery was a tiny hard-won triumph, a reminder that even in a digital world, the smallest physical details could hold the key to everything.

LESSONS IN LEADERSHIP

This crisis became a defining moment in my career, reinforcing my conviction in the power of teamwork, creative problem-solving, and the importance of trusting people to rise to challenges. The experience also shaped my leadership philosophy—one that values flexibility, persistence, and collaboration as the cornerstones of success.

The WWMCCS/JOPES failure during Desert Storm was a test of resilience and leadership. We entered the crisis unsure of how to recover, but by sparking innovation and leaning on the team's diverse talents, we transformed a potential disaster into a resounding success. This chapter in my career redefined how I approached problem-solving and reinforced the idea that with determination and ingenuity, even the toughest challenges can be overcome.

A RESTLESS AMBITION

At forty years old, a restless ambition simmered inside me. I stood in my cubicle, staring at a report that quantified progress but lacked vision. Leading software development and maintenance teams was rewarding but, by then, routine. Adequate, but not enough to ignite the sense of purpose I craved. I wanted to make a broader impact by shaping policies and influencing change. The horizon no longer stretched far enough; I had to climb higher.

The Air Force, with its constant presence in my life since childhood, felt natural, almost inevitable, as my next challenge. Growing up near Scott Air Force Base, my father's stories of weather radar programs and Pentagon adventures planted seeds in me that, years later, blossomed into a desire to aid this institution on a grander scale. If I could secure a Senior Executive

Service role in the Air Force, I would bring my accumulated experiences full circle, shaping policy for the same organization that shaped my youth.

And so, with a sense of purpose and determination, I set my sights on that peak, ready to take on the challenges, seize the opportunities, and leave my mark.

But how does one stand out in a sea of talented individuals, all vying for a coveted spot in the Senior Executive Service? How could I demonstrate my technical expertise and management experience in a larger way with the Air Force's missions?

The answer was right in front of me—civilian training.

FINAL PIECE OF THE SES PUZZLE

The Civilian Training Requirements System was the final piece in my SES preparation puzzle. The CTRS showcased my ability to think strategically and solve complex organizational challenges in a way that few others had attempted. By transforming a long-overlooked issue into a data-driven initiative, I demonstrated the kind of forward-thinking leadership and innovation that directly aligned with the Executive Core Qualifications (ECQs) required for Senior Executive Service positions. From leading change and building coalitions to results-driven decision-making, my career achievements up to that point checked every box.

Through CTRS, I had proven my capacity for vision by translating a critical need into a practical solution that elevated our mission readiness. This, coupled with years of experience navigating operational challenges and implementing large-scale initiatives, had prepared me for leadership at the highest level. And the timing couldn't have been better. My contributions had not gone unnoticed; Air Force leadership now saw me as someone with the drive, acumen, and ability to address issues with lasting impact.

I knew I was ready to compete successfully for an SES position. My career thus far had equipped me with the skills, experience, and strategic perspective to step into this role with confidence. With the support of leadership and a clear grasp of what it would take to thrive at this next level, I felt momentum building. I was prepared to make an even greater contribution to advancing the mission, leading in complex environments, and shaping the future of public service.

And as if fate had orchestrated it, within weeks of CTRS's completion, an SES vacancy opened at the Headquarters of the US Air Force in the Pentagon. The position? Executive Director of Architecture, Technology, and Interoperability, the highest-ranking civilian position for information technology in the Air Force. The opportunity perfectly aligned with my skills and aspirations. I was ready to seize the moment and applied. The application process was rigorous, the competition fierce. But I had a story to tell, a story of innovation, and a lifetime commitment to the Air Force and its mission.

And that story resonated. After a series of interviews and evaluations, I received the news I had been hoping for: I was selected for the SES position. This was a moment of immense satisfaction, a validation of years of hard work and dedication. With a mix of excitement and anticipation, I prepared to embark on this new chapter, trading my familiar cubicle for the halls of the Pentagon, ready to lead at the highest levels of the Air Force.

PART IV

SENIOR EXECUTIVE SERVICE

FROM THE PENTAGON TO VETERANS AFFAIRS

Part IV represents the crescendo of my career—a path that led me through the halls of power, moments of deep self-reflection, and ultimately back to a mission I was destined to serve. It's a story of pushing boundaries and stepping into roles where the stakes were monumental and the rewards deeply personal. From influencing policy at the Pentagon to leading transformative change at the Department of Veterans Affairs, these chapters unveil the highs and lows of navigating leadership at the highest levels, where every decision could ripple across thousands of lives.

In this section, I move beyond achievements to focus on discovery. You'll join me as I confront the pull between innovation and tradition, confront the unexpected challenges of the private sector, and find a renewed sense of purpose by answering a call that's bigger than any individual. Part IV offers more than a glimpse into boardrooms and strategy meetings, bringing you to the heart of what it means to serve, adapt, and remain true to your values in a rapidly changing world.

CHAPTER 8

DIGITAL HIGHWAYS

THE PENTAGON

"The power of excellence is overwhelming. It is always in demand, and nobody cares about its color."

—GENERAL DANIEL "CHAPPIE" JAMES JR., USAF

This quote from General Chappie James, the first African American four-star General in the United States Air Force, speaks to the importance of striving for excellence, regardless of one's background. It resonates with my experiences in the Pentagon, where I first served in the Senior Executive Service. This chapter explores the challenges of leading at the strategic level, shaping policy, and navigating the political landscape, all while striving to uphold the highest standards of service and integrity.

When	1995	1996	1997
Rank	\multicolumn{3}{c}{Senior Executive Service}		
Location	\multicolumn{3}{c}{US Air Force Headquarters—Pentagon (DC)}		

A FIRST DAY LIKE NO OTHER

It was a cool March morning in 1995. The Pentagon's vast parking lot, a maze of asphalt and shimmering cars, stretched endlessly before me. Unlike most of the thousands who earned a daily parking battle scar, I had the luxury of access to a reserved parking area—a small perk of joining the Senior Executive Service. Soon, I spotted an empty space, heart pounding with anticipation and relief. This was my first day as a member of the headquarters Air Force "comm community" and I didn't want to be late.

The immense size of the Pentagon was both impressive and humbling. Its five sides resembled a formidable windowed fortress. As I approached, the building buzzed with activity, personnel streaming through its doors, each intent on their tasks. Inside, the high ceilings loomed above, and the polished marble floors reflected the seriousness you'd expect from the nerve center of the US military.

After I passed through security, an Air Force officer greeted me and guided me up flights of shallow, sweeping stairs. Every step on those deeply worn marble treads echoed with purpose. How many Generals, Presidents, or unsung heroes had walked this path before me? The weight of responsibility settled over me with every footfall.

Stepping out of the stairwell, I walked into a world I never expected. The stark, utilitarian corridor suddenly exploded with color and life, a striking contrast that stopped me in my tracks. Bold strokes of art and historic artifacts lined the walls, transforming the sterile passageway into a vibrant gallery.

My eyes were drawn to one painting, and the rest of the world fell away. A P-51 Mustang fighter airplane, its crimson red nose cone and tailfin ablaze against a brilliant blue sky, was frozen mid-flight, as if time itself had paused to honor it.

My heart tightened as I recognized the tribute—a celebration of the Tuskegee Airmen, the brave African American pioneers who soared through the barriers of prejudice during World War II with defiance, skill, and excellence. My childhood love for building models of this very aircraft flooded my mind.

Statues, plaques, flags, medals, and ribbons whispered of past conflicts and victories. Here, art met history, each piece of the Pentagon's eclectic tapestry honoring the people who sacrificed for this nation. This was more than a series of concrete hallways. The space functioned as an immersive museum, designed to inspire and ground those working to maintain America's defense legacy.

THE HALLWAY TO THE AIR FORCE'S DIGITAL FRONTIER

After many more twists and turns, I finally arrived at "The Hallway," a legendary corridor on the Pentagon's fifth floor where Air Force communications and information systems policy had been shaped for decades and the site of my new office. The walls were lined with pictures of the Air Force luminaries who were the architects of secure networks, guardians of vital data streams, and the pioneers of innovative solutions that empowered the Air Force's mission in an ever-evolving technological landscape.

That morning, I realized I wasn't just joining a team. I was stepping into history. The Air Force "comm community" welcomed me like family, but there was an unspoken expectation for excellence and accountability. Although I was accustomed to Air Force culture from growing up near and working at Scott Air Force Base, this experience was on a whole new level. If working at Scott was akin to high school football, this was the NFL—focused on strategy, speed, and precision.

MY PENTAGON OFFICE

The Pentagon was designed with five concentric pentagon-shaped rings (like a target) labeled A (innermost) to E (outermost). These rings were connected by corridors, enabling efficient movement and communication across the complex.

The innermost A-ring housed highly secure offices, including command centers central to defense strategies. B- and C-rings contained operational and administrative offices for managing daily defense activities. D- and E-rings hosted additional offices, support roles, and less classified functions.

The outermost E-ring was the only one with exterior views and, as a result, was home to top officials such as the Secretary of Defense and the Secretary of the Air Force.

My B-ring office on the fifth floor was a fascinating blend of old and new. A massive beige computer dominated my desk, its curved monitor glowing with the colorful icons of Windows 95, the latest operating system. Navigating this new digital landscape felt cutting-edge at the time, though in hindsight, it seems clunky and slow. But even then, there was a palpable sense of possibility in the air. On the screen, Netscape Navigator, the dominant web browser of the day, held a commanding 75 percent market share as the dot-com boom began to take hold. This dominance, however, would prove short-lived, as the internet bubble burst just five years later. Still, we were pioneers, exploring and shaping this new digital world with a sense of excitement and purpose.

My Executive Officer showed me the ropes, patiently guiding me through the archaic network login process and teaching me how to access my email (a revolutionary concept at the time). The rest of the day was a blur of introductions, orientation meetings, security briefings, and attempts to decipher the mountain of onboarding paperwork on my desk.

As I settled into my new role, I knew I had a lot to learn about the intricacies of Air Force headquarters and about the people themselves. These were individuals who had been shaped by their tours of duty around the world, forged in the fire of service, and tempered by their commitment to our nation's defense.

My first day blended awe, tradition, and motivation. Every visual detail—the polished plaques, historical artifacts, or sweeping architecture—bore witness to the Pentagon's enduring mission. These elements served as a reminder of the vital role we played, ensuring the Air Force and the nation could meet the challenges of tomorrow.

As I left for the evening, my head spinning with acronyms and protocols, I couldn't help but wonder what I had gotten myself into and whether I'd survive the bureaucratic behemoth that was the Pentagon.

NAVIGATING THE DIGITAL FRONT LINE

The post–Cold War "Peace Dividend" had ushered in significant budget reductions across the military, forcing the Air Force to make hard choices about force structure, modernization, and base closures. My role demanded creativity and strategic thinking to advance technological progress despite limited resources. Balancing efficiency with innovation, I navigated a landscape where every decision carried far-reaching implications.

This era also signaled a fundamental shift in how the Air Force approached technology and information. The lines between airpower, space, and cyberspace blurred, heralding the dawn of the information age. To meet these challenges, the Air Force embraced a bold initiative to "Operationalize and Professionalize the Network" (OPTN) in which computer networks and systems were to be treated like weapons systems.

Communications and computer personnel needed to be funded, trained, and certified with the same rigor as aircraft weapon system crews. This bold vision aimed to elevate IT infrastructure to a vital element of the digital battlespace.

The initiative to treat computer networks as weapons systems underscored the growing need for a coordinated, strategic approach to technology. This realization marked a turning point in my career, as I shifted focus from hands-on IT innovation to shaping the policies that would support and sustain the Air Force's technological progress on a larger scale.

FROM CODE TO POLICY

My mission was to create policy, not code.

This was strategy at its highest level, a role where decisions rippled across the entire Air Force organization. My task was clear but formidable: to develop Air Force–wide policies, ensuring a broad architecture framework with seamless interoperability of computers and communication systems.

These systems were the lifeline of the Air Force's global missions, and achieving cohesion within such a diverse organization meant more than aligning technology; it required building bridges between people, ideas, and entrenched processes.

I also served as the civilian leader of the Air Force Civilian Career Program, which set the standards for recruiting, education, training, and career-broadening assignments for civilians in the Air Force's computers and communications program, which is where my Civilian Training Requirements System proved invaluable.

The language of policy itself presented a new challenge: I needed to write with clarity, concision, and persuasion, while also considering the legal and ethical implications that weren't part of my IT experience. The problems I encountered were no longer neatly solvable code blocks; instead, they required me to zoom out and understand how different parts of the Air Force organization interacted. Unlike code, success in policy creation wasn't a simple "it works" or "it doesn't." It meant mitigating risk, improving compliance, and achieving those elusive organizational goals that are hard to measure. This shift forced me to confront ambiguity head-on and develop my communication skills.

The transition from software to policy creation was daunting, but ultimately, it broadened my perspective and helped me appreciate the strategic side of things. I learned to see beyond the technology itself and grasp the bigger picture—how a single policy could have far-reaching implications throughout the entire system. By embracing this new reality, I gained a deeper understanding of the "why" behind the rules.

THE CHALLENGE OF INTEROPERABILITY

At the core of my role was the need to create a shared vision among the Air Force's major commands. Each command operated with its own culture, systems, and mission priorities (different horses for different courses), which made creating a unified approach to interoperability akin to solving a sprawling puzzle. For example, the fighter pilots of Air Combat Command, with their swagger and need for speed, inhabited a different world from the logistics experts of Air Force Materiel Command, whose mission was to research, acquire, and maintain Air Force weapon systems.

Success hinged on buy-in from leaders across the Air Force. I quickly realized that behind every system and policy decision were thousands of men and women relying on effective communication and computing systems to execute their missions, both in the skies and on the ground.

I took a strategic approach by reaching out to stakeholders across the major commands to understand their unique challenges. This feedback informed a framework that emphasized flexibility while setting standards for the development and integration of systems. Whether it was communications during critical missions or the management of everyday data flows, the policies had to stand up to scrutiny and deliver reliability under pressure.

INVESTING IN THE FUTURE

Serving as the leader of the Air Force Civilian Career Program for the computers and communications career field was one of the most impactful aspects of my Pentagon assignment, offering the chance to define how civilian talent was recruited, trained, and empowered. My mission was clear—to create meaningful paths for civilians to gain the skills and experiences needed to excel. I introduced more structured programs, encouraged rotational assignments across major commands, and implemented training initiatives to keep pace with rapidly emerging technologies like the internet. This work built a civilian workforce ready to meet the Air Force's future challenges.

Every time I left my three-star boss's office, I'd catch my reflection in a brass plaque beside the door that read, "Never attribute to maliciousness that which is attributable to ignorance." To me, this was a call to action. The meaning was clear. Don't assume that people are trying to be mean when they struggle with a task you haven't trained them to do. It was *my* job to ensure others had the training and tools needed to succeed. That small plaque influenced my leadership style and how I approached challenges—with empathy and a belief in best intentions.

THE TOTAL FORCE CONCEPT

This belief was essential in fostering the Air Force's "Total Force" concept, where civilians worked seamlessly alongside active duty, Guard, and Reserve personnel. Civilians brought continuity and fresh perspectives that were critical to advancing the mission. Investing in their training meant preparing for the future. Readiness was about supporting the people who carried it out, ensuring they had the foundation to thrive in a fast-changing environment.

One of the most memorable examples of this collaborative effort came during a meeting at Randolph Air Force Base. We gathered at the Air Force Personnel Center to discuss how best to utilize the growing power of the World Wide Web to enhance recruitment. The internet was still a growing tool, and recruitment strategies were being redefined. The lively energy in the room was undeniable as we debated keywords like "innovation" and "opportunity" to help recruits find our webpage in internet searches. Then, an unexpected revelation surfaced. "Sex" had topped online search words. The room went silent until the General broke it with a wry smile. "Well, I think we can all agree that one's not going to make the cut."

While the moment was lighthearted, the discussion was meaningful. Recruiting civilians through the internet meant finding language that resonated with ambition, possibility, and purpose. This approach mirrored a larger shift in the Air Force, blending tradition with innovation to stay ahead in a rapidly modernizing world.

THE GREAT SPECIMEN CUP SHORTAGE

The Pentagon in 1996 was a labyrinth of high-stakes decisions, endless corridors, and a bureaucracy so dense it sometimes felt like satire. My role put me right at the intersection of innovation and tradition, a vantage point that often came with its quirks, like the day a drug test turned into a tale for the ages.

It began abruptly with a call from my boss's assistant instructing me to report to the General's office *immediately*. In the Pentagon, *immediately* is not a suggestion, so I bolted down the corridor. The General's secretary greeted me with the kind of calm that only comes from decades of having seen it all. Her tilted head toward the door offered all the context I needed.

Inside, the General fixed me with a look of gravity typically reserved for a red switch communications failure. "You've been selected for a random drug test. Report to the clinic—now!"

Relief hit me like a wave. The urgency wasn't due to some E-ring protocol misstep I had committed. I barked, "Yes, Sir," perhaps too formally for what ultimately boiled down to peeing into a cup. Unsure where the clinic even was, I asked to borrow his Executive Officer for directions, and the General obliged.

The Exec, precise and swift, set a pace through the Pentagon's endless maze of identical corridors that rivaled professional racewalkers. We weaved through twist after twist until we reached the clinic, where, without a word, he turned heel and headed back toward his own duties.

Inside, the clinic was unnervingly quiet. A Specialist handed me some paperwork and stepped out to retrieve a specimen cup. Time ticked by. Five minutes passed. The wait became too curious to ignore, so I poked my head out and asked, "Everything okay out there?"

The Specialist returned, visibly sheepish. "Sir, I'm sorry, but we've run out of civilian specimen cups. We only have military ones, and those aren't authorized for civilian use."

Civilian specimen cups? My mind flooded with ridiculous possibilities. Could there really be design differences? Did civilian cups have soft edges? Did military cups come in camo, with tiny embellishments like anchors or grenades? I imagined Air Force cups—high-tech and titanium reinforced. The absurdity was as rich as it was baffling. I kept a straight face, nodded, and headed back to report the news.

The General listened, raised an eyebrow, then shifted his gaze to the Exec, who confirmed the bizarre twist. For a moment, the General looked tempted to make a joke about proper cup sizes for civilians but instead handed me a staff summary sheet dripping with red edits and waved me off.

And so, I became an unwitting participant in the Great Specimen Cup Shortage of 1996—a perfect illustration of how Pentagon bureaucracy could turn even the mundane into a bureaucratic punch line. Amid the high-stakes seriousness of defense operations, moments like these offered rare levity in the sometimes absurd dance of tradition, innovation, and red tape.

BUILDING RELATIONSHIPS

My days in The Hallway began earlier than most. Pentagon life had a rhythm of its own, starting way before dawn and stretching into long hours of intense activity. I had always been an early riser, probably attributable to my father's farming roots. Every day, I made early "morning rounds," a practice I developed to build connections across the Air Force's organizational pillars. The walk from my office to the other Air Force Deputy Chiefs of Staff such as Operations, Logistics, Acquisition, Finance, and Personnel became my personal circuit.

These interactions were deliberate and strategic. By fostering early-morning relationships with secretaries, executive officers, and admin staff, I gained firsthand insights into each organization's challenges and priorities. These connections helped create a network of trust that I drew upon as I worked to align policy and operational goals. Over time, this relationship-building practice proved invaluable. This approach ensured I could avoid roadblocks and rally support or better understand the opposition about issues across organizational silos, even in the face of difficult policy changes or new initiatives. My morning rounds were not merely a social (and physical) exercise. They laid the foundation for cohesive action across the Air Force's diverse landscape.

ENHANCING INTEROPERABILITY ACROSS THE AIR FORCE

At the heart of my role was one of the Air Force's most complex challenges: interoperability. My goal was to align the Air Force's eleven major commands and thousands of systems, ensuring a unified framework for effective communication and coordination. This was no small task. The Air Force's network of people, processes, and technologies spanned a global operational theater. Ensuring interoperability not only required technical expertise but also organizational alignment and cultural transformation.

One of the most formidable challenges I faced was fostering an *enterprise* mindset. The Air Force was undergoing a critical evolution, shifting from fragmented, tribally isolated islands of information to a state of complete connectivity. This vision demanded not only a unified approach to technology but also a cultural and organizational shift that embraced a broader, enterprise-wide perspective.

Comprehensive compliance became a nonnegotiable element of this effort, ensuring security and reliability across the interconnected systems. Our Pentagon office was ably supported by the Air Force Communications Agency at Scott AFB, which offered the technical insights and support necessary to propel this enterprise mindset forward.

TECHNICAL AND ORGANIZATIONAL HURDLES

Technically, the hurdles were daunting. Many outdated systems in the Air Force couldn't work well with newer technologies, causing delays and poor communication. Without shared standards, fixes were often isolated and didn't solve bigger problems.

Organizationally, the stovepiped approach to system development hindered progress. Projects were often designed without considering how they'd fit into the bigger picture, leaving scattered systems that didn't connect well. This reactive way of working drained resources and slowed momentum. Shifting from this reactive cycle to a proactive one required a cultural change to embed interoperability principles at every step.

To meet these challenges, standardization was essential. The Department of Defense Architecture Framework (DoDAF) provided the structure we needed to ensure consistency in how systems were designed, developed, and deployed. Aligning with DoDAF principles allowed us to prioritize mission needs while creating the foundation for a coherent, interconnected system.

SIMPLIFYING COMPLEXITY WITH LEGOS

The Department of Defense Architecture Framework was a critical tool for advancing interoperability within the Air Force and DOD. The framework outlined three related architectural viewpoints—Operational Architecture, System Architecture, and Technical Architecture—each essential for aligning mission goals with communications and computers capabilities. But understanding this framework was like trying to grasp a handful of sand—the more you squeezed, the more it slipped away.

To unlock understanding and adoption, I needed to create something simple and tangible. I wanted to give people the opportunity to learn through their fingers, like I did. So, I raided my kids' toy box for a stash of LEGO blocks and set out to build a model that could make sense of the three architectural viewpoints: Operational, System, and Technical Architecture.

The finished model comprised a white plastic box with three different-colored drawers. Each drawer represented one of the three DoDAF architectural viewpoints. The bottom blue drawer symbolized the Technical Architecture, the middle red drawer captured the System Architecture, and the top yellow drawer illustrated the Operational Architecture. By physically pulling out each drawer, I could talk about what belonged inside each drawer and show how these layers supported one another.

This LEGO model transformed the abstract "snoozer" DoDAF into a hands-on tool that audiences could understand. Their heads were nodding, not nodding off. By visualizing the architectural layers and their relationships, stakeholders gained clarity on the strategic importance of DoDAF. This innovative approach not only made the framework accessible but also galvanized support for its adoption, enabling the Air Force to better manage system complexity, achieve mission alignment, and enhance operational precision.

IMPLEMENTING THE CLINGER-COHEN ACT AND PREPARING FOR Y2K

Beyond interoperability and architecture, some of my most impactful challenges involved grappling with pressing legislative and technical mandates. One of these was the implementation of the Federal Information Technology Management Reform Act (ITMRA), also known as the Clinger-Cohen Act.

The Clinger-Cohen Act, introduced as part of the National Defense Authorization Act of 1996, marked a significant overhaul in government IT management. Designed to streamline IT acquisitions and prioritize life-cycle management as a capital investment, the act transformed procurement practices across federal agencies. The new law made agency heads directly responsible for acquiring and managing IT investments, requiring each agency to demonstrate that funded technology projects would improve processes, enhance efficiency, and reduce costs.

A key feature of the act was the requirement for each executive agency to appoint a Chief Information Officer (CIO) that reported to the Secretary of that agency. The introduction of dedicated CIO roles ensured closer alignment of IT systems with organizational objectives, while also providing a centralized authority to oversee technology investments and operations.

For the Department of Defense and the Air Force, the Clinger-Cohen Act proved particularly impactful. Since managing IT investments was a central part of the Act, the Air Force named its Assistant Secretary for Acquisition to the role of CIO, tasked with coordinating IT projects and breaking down "stovepiped" system silos. However, my office served a central role in the creation of policy for its operational implementation.

I became a staunch advocate for the CIO role, focused on helping stakeholders see IT not merely as a functional tool but as a strategic enabler for mission success.

Simultaneously, the looming Y2K crisis demanded urgent attention. Managing the Y2K crisis at Air Force headquarters was an intense, high-stakes endeavor. The Air Force's heavy reliance on technology meant that any failure, from fighter jets to communication systems, could risk mission readiness. The root of the issue, a decades-old programming shortcut using two-digit date fields, left systems vulnerable to interpreting "00" as 1900. As a former software coder, I knew exactly how dangerous Y2K was.

AVERTING DISASTER

In fact, the potential risks were considered so severe that the Air Force hosted Russian counterparts in a Y2K center to ensure that a turn-of-the-millennium computer error wouldn't spark a catastrophic nuclear security incident. This unprecedented cooperation underscored the gravity of those years and the immense responsibility we bore to safeguard global stability.

Coordinating the Air Force Communications Agency and the Y2K Program Management Office, we adopted a phased approach—raising awareness, assessing vulnerabilities, renovating code, validating fixes, and implementing solutions.

Air Force budget constraints and the exodus of skilled personnel (especially COBOL programmers) to higher-paying jobs forced tough decisions. Delaying nonessential upgrades and reallocating resources ensured our focus on critical systems.

The pressure was immense, but on January 1, 2000, our efforts paid off. Mission-critical systems functioned as intended, a validation of months of relentless work. Reflecting back, managing Y2K was more than a technical victory. The effort safeguarded confidence in the Air Force's mission, proving the power of teamwork and preparation in the face of daunting challenges.

TECHNOLOGY AT THE HELM: LOOKING AHEAD

Before my arrival in the Pentagon, the Air Force had made a groundbreaking choice and appointed a renowned computer scientist, not a traditional aeronautical expert, to serve as its Chief Scientist. This visionary wasn't just any run-of-the-mill computer scientist; he was a trailblazer in artificial intelligence (AI), widely regarded as one of the founding figures of the field.

A SCIENTIST'S VISION

This appointment signaled the Air Force's understanding that the nature of warfare was evolving. Traditional air superiority was no longer enough. Success in modern conflicts would require dominance in data and the seamless integration of advanced information technology. The Chief Scientist's expertise brought a fresh vision to the table, positioning the Air Force to lead in air, space, and cyberspace.

What heightened this experience for me were the opportunities I had to interact with him. Discussing ideas with such a pioneering mind was invigorating, reinforcing the sense that I had a front-row seat to the future of digital innovation in defense.

I recall a striking moment that underscored his visionary approach. During a conversation, we discussed the potential use of PDF files as a way of exchanging outputs from software programs rather than paper printouts. A PDF, or Portable Document Format, is a file format designed to preserve the layout of a document, regardless of the device displaying it. Though ubiquitous today, PDFs were considered an innovation in the Pentagon at the time.

His enthusiasm for (what he viewed as) simple advancements like PDFs was inspiring; he understood that even seemingly small innovations could deliver outsized results when applied strategically. That conversation crystallized for me the magnitude of his appointment and the power of innovation to redefine what was possible and what would be necessary for the future of national defense.

A CIVILIAN IN A MILITARY WORLD

Working as a civilian employee in a military environment offered a unique perspective, especially within the Pentagon's disciplined and mission-driven atmosphere. While civilians and military personnel shared a common goal of defending the nation, our roles were distinct. Military members, bound by the Uniform Code of Military Justice (UCMJ), followed strict protocols that governed everything from their professional conduct to personal fitness and appearance. Their oath of office carried the weight of potentially making the ultimate sacrifice, an unwavering sense of duty that permeated every aspect of the mission.

For civilians like me, the service was different but equally vital. We weren't subject to the same rigorous rules as military members, yet our expertise and continuity were critical to mission success. My role often complemented the operational focus of my military colleagues, and I witnessed firsthand the risks civilians faced, particularly in high-stakes or deployed environments. These contributions, although distinct from those of military personnel, reinforced our importance to the larger mission.

ADAPTING TO MILITARY CULTURE

To succeed in DOD, adapting to military culture was essential. Having grown up in a Southern Illinois town steeped in Air Force culture, where "Yes, sir" and "No, ma'am" were the default responses to any adult, the structured chain of command and formal communication felt natural to me. Though I wasn't bound by the UCMJ, I worked to align my actions and approach with military values, further developing my profound respect for their way of life. Over time, I found a sense of belonging and pride, deeply connected to their mission and shared principles.

What stood out most was the unified sense of purpose. Regardless of whether we were military or civilian, we were bound by a commitment to protect the nation. My civilian role didn't require combat training or strategic battlefield knowledge, yet my contributions fit into the larger whole, enhancing the mission's success. That shared dedication became a badge of honor for me—a reminder of the pride I felt in serving alongside those I deeply respected.

To this day, I carry that sense of purpose and respect with me, grateful for the opportunity to support national defense and honored to have stood, in my own way, alongside the dedicated men and women in uniform.

A FORMATIVE CRUCIBLE

The Pentagon was the most challenging assignment in my entire career. Never had I been asked to put more of myself into my job. Never had more been expected of me. Never had I felt so deeply the weight of responsibility. Through the challenges I faced and the lessons I learned, I came to deeply value collaboration, vision, and adaptability. Navigating its labyrinthine halls and juggling its high-stakes priorities was exhausting and exhilarating. But it was that pressure, and the opportunity to rise to the occasion and be held accountable, that left a lasting mark on me.

The incredible leaders I had the privilege to work with and learn from during my tenure left an indelible mark on my career and personal development. The Generals, Colonels, and civilians who led the Air Force headquarters IT organization embodied its core values of Integrity First, Service Before Self, and Excellence in All We Do. They demonstrated the true meaning of servant leadership—a commitment to putting the needs of others before one's own, even when it meant making difficult decisions or sacrifices.

For a time, I walked the same halls as the giants of military and national service. I strove to contribute something meaningful to that legacy, shaping policies, systems, and frameworks that would enable the Air Force to not only meet the challenges of the day but to thrive far into the future.

A TROUBLING QUESTION

Reflecting on my time at the Pentagon, I see a period marked by purpose and unity. Side by side with extraordinary teams and visionary leaders, we bridged the divide between technology, people, and mission goals, creating a cohesive whole that delivered on its promise. But as I immersed myself in the Pentagon's intricate systems and witnessed the unrelenting strain of its budget cuts, a troubling question began to surface. The stark reality of DOD financial strains felt far more than academic, striking at something deeply personal. I began to question the long-term stability of my civil service retirement pension, a worry that took root and began to shadow my sense of security. These concerns didn't just linger; they fueled a profound reckoning that would shape my next steps. The leadership, strategic thinking, and problem-solving skills I had honed during those years, however, became my compass as I ventured into uncharted waters—the fast-paced, high-stakes world of private sector information technology services.

CHAPTER 9

THE LONG ROAD BACK TO PURPOSE

"*Success is not final, failure is not fatal: it is the courage to continue that counts.*"

—WINSTON CHURCHILL

This quote from Churchill perfectly captures the spirit of Chapter 9, where I navigated the challenges and uncertainties of the private sector after leaving the familiar world of civil service. It was a time of both setbacks and triumphs, requiring me to adapt, innovate, and persevere in a demanding and competitive environment. This chapter explores the lessons I learned about resilience, the importance of building relationships, and the courage to embrace new opportunities, even when the path forward is uncertain.

When	1997	2002	2007	2012	2016
Rank	SES	\multicolumn{4}{c}{Private Sector VP of IT Services}	
Location	Pentagon	\multicolumn{4}{c}{Washington, DC}	

THE CALL TO LEAVE CIVIL SERVICE

My pension projections stared back at me like cracks spreading across a once-solid foundation. I sat at my desk, staring at the numbers, the once-reassuring figures now casting doubt over my future. The Civil Service Retirement System I had trusted for decades felt increasingly fragile, like a fence beginning to buckle under too much weight. Suddenly, the retirement security I had taken for granted seemed more like thin scaffolding over a deep chasm, ready to give way with the next big wind of government budget tightening. The realization hit hard—that the promises underpinning years of dedicated service might crumble before I could reap the benefits.

The political momentum behind the Federal Workforce Restructuring Act was a harsh reality check. The goal of cutting 273,000 federal jobs made it abundantly clear to me that my years of service and dedication didn't really matter. I felt like nothing more than a number on a balance sheet, an easy target for efficiency measures and deficit reduction. Coupled with constant budget cuts and relentless talk of government waste, it left me questioning the value of my work and the future of my career.

What made it even worse was the support for this Act by congressional representatives from Virginia and Maryland, whose districts were populated with significant numbers of government workers like me. Their decision felt like a personal betrayal, a move that showed just how little protection we had. I worried that the civil service pension fund, something I depended on for my future, would be raided to pay off government debt. The lack of political will to safeguard it was patently obvious. This financial uncertainty weighed heavily on me. I couldn't ignore the possibility that everything I had worked for, my pension, my stability, could vanish.

At the same time, the private sector, fueled by the dot-com boom, was exploding with opportunity. Seeing so much growth, innovation, and potential happening outside of government felt intoxicating. The contrast was undeniable. While I was stuck grappling with fears about my financial stability and the eroding support for civil servants, the private sector seemed full of promise and possibility. That stark difference became impossible to ignore.

But the cracks weren't just financial. I felt a quiet, more insidious shift happening around me within the Department of Defense. Budget cuts from the post–Cold War "Peace Dividend" were stripping away resources, and an unspoken hierarchy was sowing division between military and civilian employees.

A LUNCHTIME EPIPHANY

I remember one day vividly—a lunch at the General Officer's dining hall. The dining hall in the Pentagon was familiar territory. I'd eaten there many times before. After all, my SES position was the civilian equivalent rank of a two-star General. But this time, something felt different. The room, sparsely filled with a few seated Brigadier Generals, was quiet enough that every clink of silverware sounded amplified. The white tablecloths and polished place settings gleamed as always, yet an almost imperceptible shift in the atmosphere hung heavily.

Perhaps it was the stress of budget cuts looming over every Air Force program. Perhaps it was a bad traffic Monday after a Redskins loss at DC's RFK Stadium.

Perhaps it was my imagination.

But it wasn't.

The professionalism of the room was intact yet detached, like a machine running on precision without warmth.

I walked to a table, heels softly tapping the floor, glances flickering toward me before darting away. I adjusted my posture as my chair creaked beneath me, trying to blend in, though I felt like I was sitting just outside the picture frame. Dining room staff moved efficiently, the hushed hum of the room underscored by soft murmurs at distant tables.

But the glances said it all. Career civilians didn't belong here.

It was a small slight, insignificant to the onlookers, but to me, the moment crystallized something I had been trying not to confront. Despite my years of hard work and devotion, my contributions were seen as secondary. I was part of the system, but not truly embraced by it.

A DIFFICULT DECISION

Financial concerns and small moments like these accumulated and began to chip away at the confidence I had once placed in my career. The erosion wasn't immediate. A slow, steady realization crept in that the future financial foundation I had built my life upon might not hold. I wrestled with an internal storm—my devotion to the mission and everything it represented, clashing with a growing unease about how I could prepare for my family's future within a system that felt increasingly fractured.

Leaving was never the easy choice; it felt like both a retreat from a world I loved and a leap into one I feared. I agonized over financial scenarios late into the night, chasing the numbers for clarity I couldn't seem to find. Walking away from civil service was a release of the identity I had spent decades cultivating, requiring me to relinquish the stability I depended on and face an uncertain future. But as much as it pained me to leave, I couldn't ignore the signs any longer. This was not the same civil service I had started in, and the dreams I'd tied to it no longer felt secure.

LEAVING THE PENTAGON

On my last day at the Pentagon, I took one final look back at the building that had reshaped me. I knew about the common going-away gift—a framed picture of a car's rearview mirror with the Pentagon in it. But I wanted no part of that sentiment.

To me, the Pentagon had never been something to escape. I loved it. My heart pounded when I walked the E-ring, passing portraits of leaders who gave so much of themselves to serve with unparalleled impact. I admired their sacrifices, loved the defense mission that united us all, thrived in the relentless pace, and marveled at the art that lined its halls.

Leaving wasn't driven by bitterness but by necessity—a need to explore the private sector to secure my financial future. The decision was a test of my mettle, not a rejection of what I cherished.

As I stepped away into uncertainty that day, I carried the Pentagon's ideals with me: purpose, dedication, camaraderie. The moment wasn't a goodbye but a recalibration, a moment to gather strength for whatever lay ahead. My Pentagon time became my foundation, steadying me as I faced the unknown with determination and the promise of transformation.

BRIDGING TWO WORLDS

Transitioning from government service to the private sector was like stepping onto a racetrack defined by rapid decisions, intense competition, and an unrelenting pace. My Blackberry mobile phone became my constant companion, buzzing with emails and calls at all hours. After years of working in structured environments with long-term mission objectives, I found myself navigating an entirely new world driven by short-term measurable results and adaptability. Though tumultuous at first, this shift became a defining chapter in my career—one where I leveraged my expertise in Air Force technology and my deep understanding of the Department of Defense to redefine how IT could support national defense priorities.

The Air Force technology market provided a solid foundation as I embraced the private sector's dynamics. Having honed my knowledge through years of civil service, I entered the Federal System Integrator space confidently, knowing I could provide unique value. These companies were pivotal partners for the government, entrusted with transforming complex IT infrastructures to meet critical deadlines. Their work demanded not just technical solutions but also an acute awareness of and alignment with federal mission priorities.

RESHAPING GOVERNMENT IT

My role in these companies centered on reshaping government IT operations. The turn of the century ushered in immense technological advancements and globalization, sparking a revolution in IT outsourcing. Within the DOD, where draconian budget cuts were straining both resources and mission readiness, IT outsourcing surfaced as a strategic enabler. Companies like IBM, EDS, CSC, Perot Systems, and others had already proven the commercial success of IT outsourcing models, offering manufacturing CFOs significant up-front financial payments plus 30 percent annual cost savings of their IT operations. I saw an opportunity to adapt and advocate for these solutions within the federal landscape, specifically for the Air Force and DOD sectors.

My firsthand experience with DOD IT operations and my (personal) understanding of Air Force budget pressures positioned me to effectively bridge the gap between the private sector's capabilities and the military's unique needs. I framed IT outsourcing as a tool to reallocate savings toward critical defense objectives, ensuring efficiency without compromising mission readiness. My work involved tailoring proposals that balanced technological innovation with budget realities, speaking directly to the priorities of military leadership.

THE ART OF THE PITCH

Crafting these strategies required technical expertise, storytelling, and relationship building. For instance, in my briefings to Air Force stakeholders, I simplified complex IT outsourcing concepts into actionable plans that aligned with their mission-driven goals. Drawing on the Tom Peters management principle of "stick to your knitting," I emphasized that the Air Force should invest its scarce resources in its core mission—air superiority—and rely on the private sector (read: my company) to provide commodity IT products and services. Each initiative showcased measurable outcomes, such as improved IT system reliability and speed at lower cost, reinforcing the value of staying true to the Air Force's strategic strengths.

NAVIGATING THE PRIVATE SECTOR

The fast pace of the private sector pushed me well beyond my comfort zone, presenting challenges I embraced and ultimately thrived in. In this environment, every decision carried financial implications, every presentation required precision, and every client interaction became an opportunity. This high-stakes setting sharpened my ability to adapt, communicate, and deliver results under pressure.

A MENTOR IN THE PRIVATE SECTOR

My first supervisor played a pivotal role in shaping how I approached these challenges. He was a master at balancing technical expertise with the art of persuasive communication. His office itself was a reflection of his multifaceted personality and career. The walls displayed his legacy—gleaming industry awards in polished wood and sleek metal celebrated his professional achievements, while military mementos spoke to his heritage as part of a distinguished Army family. Framed photographs, carefully placed models, and a striking collection of challenge coins told the story of his connection to service and tradition. Each coin—medallions exchanged for special achievements or significant visits—offered a glimpse into his vast network and the respect he had earned across various ventures.

Amid this decor, his sense of humor stood out as much as his accomplishments, most evident in the poster hanging behind his desk—a rustic cabin set in a woodland scene, emblazoned with the words, "You can't shoot a moose while sitting in the lodge." That quirky statement was his mantra and the most valuable piece of advice I received in the private sector. The meaning was clear and practical: Success required more than competence or data. Proactive personal engagement, the cultivation of genuine relationships, and the ability to craft a compelling story that resonated with clients were essential. Winning contracts required quoting a reasonably low price and connecting solutions to client goals in meaningful ways delivered through a channel of earned trust. In effect, I had to win the contract before the Request for Proposal was released.

BUILDING TRUST

From his guidance, I quickly learned a timeless principle in business: "People buy from people they trust." Trust became the linchpin of my approach. Whether positioning for upcoming contracts, presenting solutions, or navigating challenging client needs, my focus was on demonstrating consistency, understanding, and integrity. Delivering results was important, but the true goal was building enduring partnerships rooted in mutual confidence and aligned objectives.

This approach proved indispensable when I worked with clients like the Air Force. They operated under immense pressure, balancing the dual demands of shrinking budgets and critical missions. Their need for IT solutions that were "faster, better, and cheaper" presented a formidable challenge.

Merging creativity with the structured expectations of the public sector became my hallmark, enabling me to bridge the gap between innovative ideas and practical outcomes that truly resonated with clients. By combining innovation with diplomacy, I translated complex outsourcing concepts into strategies that aligned with their goals. My ability to frame these solutions with respect to their constraints and a clear path forward set me apart. I learned to align innovations with customer requirements and mission imperatives.

THE VALUE OF PUBLIC AND PRIVATE PARTNERSHIPS

Working at the intersection of the public and private sectors revealed a truth I hadn't fully appreciated before. These two worlds, often seen as opposites, were indispensable to one another. The opportunities I pursued and the projects I managed for the Air Force weren't just about managing technology or meeting contract deliverables. They were about something bigger: serving national missions. This realization transformed how I approached my role, turning it from a job into a calling.

The private sector taught me strategic thinking on a scale I hadn't experienced in government. Federal contracting demanded meticulous alignment with regulations like the Federal Acquisition Regulation (FAR) while simultaneously requiring creativity and problem-solving to meet client needs. The delicate balance between adherence to strict protocols and delivering impactful results heightened my ability to think critically and pivot quickly.

Take, for example, crafting proposals for Air Force initiatives. Each proposal required a deep understanding of technological challenges and broader mission objectives. I needed to tell a story that positioned our work as indispensable to the Air Force's strategic goals. This blend of storytelling, negotiation, and technical foresight was a skill I carried with me back into public service later in my career.

Beyond strategy, I learned that navigating federal partnerships required trust, transparency, and shared values. Success came from consistently delivering results and aligning with the mission, whether deploying IT systems or leading large-scale projects. The private sector also introduced me to a network of motivated, talented individuals and companies whose varied perspectives sparked innovation and learning. These connections evolved into a valuable professional web I relied on throughout my career.

A SYNTHESIS OF STRENGTHS

Perhaps the most profound lesson was understanding how the strengths of the private and public sectors could be synthesized. The private world's drive toward innovation and urgency complemented the public sector's focus on stability, service, and long-term impact. Working in both realms allowed me to see these synergies in action—how streamlined technology systems, crafted with private-sector ingenuity, could empower government agencies to excel in their missions and lay the groundwork for sustained future success.

These lessons reframed my perspective on what it meant to serve. I came to see my role not as working for the government or the private sector, but as part of a larger effort to bridge the two. Each conversation, each project, and each challenge strengthened my belief that purpose didn't have to be confined to one side. Instead, real impact was possible by uniting the discipline of public service with the dynamism of private enterprise.

Looking back, those years in the federal market were more than a career pivot. They were a master class in adaptability, collaboration, and understanding how to drive missions forward despite competing priorities. The experience clarified not only what I could offer but also how the interplay between public and private efforts could create something greater than either could achieve alone. This newfound clarity prepared me to return to public service with a renewed vision and an unshakable resolve to make a meaningful difference.

RENEWED PURPOSE AND PREPARING TO RETURN "HOME"

By early 2016, the thought of returning to civil service grew from a quiet whisper into a relentless pull on my heart. The private sector, while rewarding in many ways, felt adrift, its victories fleeting, its efforts unmoored from deeper meaning. I yearned for the gravity of purpose, the sense of knowing that the work mattered beyond profit or progress. I missed the mission. I longed for the hum of shared intention, the quiet but powerful knowledge that what we did shaped something larger than myself.

Years in the private sector had sharpened my resilience, strategic thinking, and adaptability. I wasn't the same person who had left the Pentagon nearly twenty years earlier. I was more prepared, clearer in my vision of how to serve effectively. The private sector had reshaped my mindset. I no longer focused solely on tasks; I now saw the bigger picture, where strategy and execution converged to create meaningful, long-term impact. I had learned the power of building partnerships, dismantling silos, and standing firm in the face of resistance. These experiences weren't just lessons; they were tools I could use to bridge the contrasting worlds of public and private sectors. The focus was on fusing these distinct strengths to contribute in a profound and innovative way.

My time in business revealed that relationships were the bedrock of success. Creativity emerged when gaps were bridged, and curiosity thrived. Yet, no matter how rewarding my private-sector work had been, my core aligned with the principles of public service: the purpose, the mission-driven focus, and the collective push toward something greater. I wanted to return, not to leave one world behind but to leverage the best of both for a greater impact.

LOOKING AHEAD TO A NEW ERA

Returning to civil service was about building something more. Armed with private-sector insights, I could see how fresh ideas and modern technologies could propel government programs to new levels while upholding accountability and stability.

The private sector taught me to innovate boldly and act with urgency, while civil service had instilled patience and long-term vision. The key lay in blending the agility of business with the enduring principles of public service.

Imagine mission-critical government programs enhanced by innovative private-sector practices or technology that served citizens with the speed and flexibility people expect today. This potential sparked my excitement and strengthened my resolve to contribute meaningfully.

Though the road ahead was uncharted, I felt ready. Leading systemic changes, inspiring collaboration, and championing modernization wouldn't be easy, but it was worth every challenge. My years away prepared me not only to adapt but to push forward with a renewed sense of purpose. This was the beginning of a new chapter filled with opportunities to help public service rise, not only to meet the future but to shape it.

CHAPTER 10

FROM LESSONS TO LEGACY

A CAREER'S CULMINATION IN SERVICE OF VETERANS

"The two most important days in your life are the day you are born and the day you find out why."

—MARK TWAIN

This quote from Twain perfectly captures the essence of Chapter 10, where I returned to public service after a long hiatus in the private sector. It was a time of rediscovering my purpose and aligning my skills with a mission that deeply resonated with my values. This chapter explores my journey at the Department of Veterans Affairs, where I found a renewed sense of meaning in leveraging technology to improve the lives of those who have served our country. It's a reflection of the transformative power of discovering your "why" and dedicating yourself to a cause that matters.

When	2016	2017	June 2018
Rank	Senior Executive Service		
Location	Dept. of Veterans Affairs (DC)		

A RENEWED SENSE OF PURPOSE

When I decided to return to the civil service, I hoped to align my professional abilities with a mission that mattered. Initially, returning to the Air Force seemed like the natural path, offering a culture of discipline and a strong connection to my past work that made it an appealing option. But a conversation with a friend working at the Department of Veterans Affairs (VA) opened up a new perspective. The VA stood for a profound mission embodied in Abraham Lincoln's promise "to care for him who shall have borne the battle and for his widow, and his orphan." For someone raised in the "Land of Lincoln," his words resonated deeply within me. Supporting Veterans—those who had sacrificed so much to protect our freedoms—felt like a calling, not just a job, and offered an opportunity to contribute to something far greater than myself.

Clarity of purpose ignites employee engagement in any organization, and at the VA this principle was deeply ingrained. Everyone, from IT professionals, who ensured systems ran smoothly; to the claims staff, who administered benefits; to the clinicians, who provided healthcare; to the memorial services team, who placed them in their final resting place recognized the profound responsibility they carried. This shared clarity fostered a unique culture of dedication. To me, the VA was a community united by a noble goal, to which I was irresistibly drawn.

JOINING THE VA

That realization brought me to the VA in October 2016, where I joined the Office of Information and Technology (OIT). Taking on this role was a professional milestone and a profound pivot in my career's narrative. Here, I saw an opportunity to leverage years of private-sector expertise to advance the VA's mission. By pairing innovation with purpose, I could help transform government operations and, more importantly, contribute directly to improving Veterans' lives.

LINCOLN'S LEGACY AS A GUIDE

On my first day at the VA, I made my way to its headquarters, just a block from the White House. The sight of the navy-blue awning at the entrance, paired with the hustle and energy of people moving inside, filled me with anticipation. Yet, it was the brass plaque on the building that stopped me in my tracks. Engraved with Lincoln's words, it stood as a powerful reminder of the commitment to serve and honor Veterans. These were individuals whose military service I had grown up admiring, supported during my career, and profoundly respected. Standing there, I felt the profound weight of this responsibility. This was more than the VA's mission; it was a deeply personal guide and would become a driving force for my work. My personal patron saint seemed to be gently urging me forward, reminding me that service is not only a duty but also the purest and most meaningful expression of leadership.

A CULTURAL SHIFT

Stepping inside, I was immediately struck by the organized energy of the place. I was ready to begin, yet something felt unfamiliar. Then it hit me. There were *no uniforms*. Coming from a long public/private sector career supporting DOD organizations, I had grown used to seeing military attire, which visually represented authority and structure. Decisions in the DOD environment followed a disciplined, straightforward process shaped by clear chains of command and mission-critical needs. The absence of such symbolism at the VA signaled something different.

This first impression highlighted a fundamental cultural shift. At the VA, respect for expertise rather than rank drove leadership. Discussions were collaboration-first, emphasizing teamwork and service-centered principles. The focus was on healthcare, benefits, and advocacy, not operational readiness. While the VA's mission was equally vital, its approach was nuanced, deeply tied to meeting Veterans' needs through cooperation and shared responsibility. The VA was more about teamwork than hierarchy.

A PERSONAL TRANSFORMATION

Adapting to this shift was not without its challenges. My DOD background had trained me to move quickly, with decisions made efficiently and cleanly through the ranks. At the VA, however, I encountered deliberation—a focus on ensuring every voice mattered, pro and con, from healthcare providers and IT employees to Veteran advocacy groups and even Congressional oversight committees. This approach wasn't fast, and initially, it tested my patience. Yet, over time, I came to see its value.

Each collaboration was a lesson in humility and service. The slower decision-making process revealed a depth of expertise and passion among the stakeholders, teaching me something I had overlooked in my former roles—patience could be a powerful strength. VA's collaborative ethos enriched my understanding of leadership, showing me that the best outcomes often emerge from collective wisdom and shared effort.

TECHNOLOGY THAT IMPROVES LIVES

Returning to civil service provided a renewed sense of purpose. Every project undertaken at the VA had a direct impact on the lives of men and women who had selflessly served the country. Unlike my prior DOD roles, the VA offered a direct connection between innovation and impact, with a clear line of sight and focus on health, benefits, and memorial services outcomes. At the VA, technology improved lives. Telehealth brought care to rural Veterans. Mobile apps streamlined claims processes and memorial affairs experiences. I could touch a kiosk in a medical center that my organization had programmed. Day after day, I witnessed technology making tangible improvements in people's lives—a reality that made my VA tenure the most fulfilling part of my entire career.

Everyone, whether managing critical IT systems or caring for Veterans, understood the weight of their task and the lives it impacted. This shared understanding fueled a culture of dedication, where every action aligned with the greater mission of serving those who have served. This dynamic made the VA a great place to work within a community bound by a singular, noble goal.

ADAPTING TO A NEW LEADERSHIP MINDSET

Transitioning from the DOD to the VA presented a significant cultural shift that redefined my approach to leadership. My time in the DOD was marked by efficiency and decisiveness, where decisions were executed with speed and precision through disciplined chains of command shaped by national security priorities. Coming to the VA, I expected a similar operational tempo, especially since many of VA's IT employees were Veterans themselves. Instead, I encountered something entirely different—a culture rooted in deliberation and nuanced service to Veterans.

This change was not easy to adapt to. VA's decision-making process resembled playing an 88-key piano, with many different stakeholders such as IT employees; the employees of VA's three primary subordinate organizations: Veterans Health Administration (VHA), the Veterans Benefits Administration (VBA), and the National Cemetery Administration (NCA); Veteran advocacy groups; Congress; and, most importantly, Veterans themselves. They all contributed their voices to the music, sometimes in discord. Meetings stretched endlessly as diverse perspectives were considered, slowing progress in ways that initially tested my patience. At times, it felt exasperating, as my ingrained DOD instincts pushed me toward quick resolutions through a chain of command. The delays weren't for their own sake but rather part of an intentional, thoughtful approach that ensured everyone was heard.

Over time, I learned to appreciate the value of this collaborative model, which focused less on speed and more on depth. Each voice, whether supportive or from ingrained constituencies resistant to change, enriched the outcomes and aligned priorities more intricately with the needs of Veterans. Patience, I realized, was a powerful strength. This richer, inclusive process pushed me to evolve as a leader, balancing decisiveness with deliberation in pursuit of outcomes that truly served the mission.

NAVIGATING POLITICAL DYNAMICS

Within the Senior Executive Service, a significant part of my role involved working closely with politically appointed leaders. At the VA, this relationship was markedly distinct from my DOD experiences. Whereas political appointees in the Pentagon operated at distant supervisory levels and rarely influenced IT decisions, the VA offered a much more interactive environment. Daily meetings, casual hallway discussions, and coffee chats with political appointees became part of my routine. These exchanges fostered a dynamic and collaborative environment, unlike the more compartmentalized structure of the DOD.

To balance these relationships, I steadfastly maintained an apolitical approach. My personal political beliefs were irrelevant. I wasn't a partisan "DC swamp monster" but a professional committed to serving Veterans. Regardless of where directives originated, my priority was always the mission's success. I consistently upheld and enforced a mission-first approach in interactions with political appointees, emphasizing that our role was to serve Veterans by executing the policies set by the Executive Branch and never to advance personal political agendas.

This commitment to nonpartisanship stemmed from my deep-seated belief that civil servants are the nonpartisan backbone of the Federal Government, providing continuity and expertise across administrations. Although civil servants must diligently implement the policies of the Executive Branch, we took an oath to uphold the Constitution, not to serve any particular political party or ideology. Our dedication was to the mission, to the American people, and to the principles of good governance. This doesn't mean we blindly followed orders; it means we offered our best advice, our objective analyses, and our commitment to serving the greater good, regardless of who sits in the Oval Office.

THE US DIGITAL SERVICE

Maintaining an apolitical, mission-first mindset was crucial in navigating the complex web of leadership dynamics within the VA. This perspective became even more essential when addressing the unique challenges brought by the US Digital Service (USDS).

The USDS, created in 2014 by President Obama, sought to enhance key government digital services, impacting federal IT innovation, particularly at the VA. However, their work at the VA exposed political and governance issues due to conflicting leadership. The VA's CIO, managing its Congressionally appropriated IT budget, reported to the VA Secretary, while USDS leadership reported to the Deputy Secretary, leading to significant tension.

The USDS engineering team, composed of talented, mostly early-career professionals, brought fresh perspectives and technical brilliance, offering bold solutions that challenged traditional "business-as-usual" mindsets. While their creativity and expertise were invaluable, their leadership's tendency to cherry-pick projects led to issues. By bypassing formal IT investment approval processes, it fostered an "us versus them" dynamic, risking perceptions of the USDS as an exclusive "cool kids' club" prioritizing high-profile projects over critical legacy system challenges.

To address this, I required USDS to choose projects from a prioritized list approved by VA's health, benefits, and memorials administrations. This approach balanced their innovative spirit with deeper stakeholder engagement, aligning their efforts with VA-wide priorities and fostering integration within the organization.

ENTERPRISE LESSONS

Stepping into VA's vast IT ecosystem, as Executive Director of the Enterprise Project Management Office (EPMO), I encountered a sprawling portfolio of over a thousand software programs, each vital to delivering healthcare and benefits to Veterans. EPMO's role was to serve as a "control tower" by managing the development and maintenance of these systems, from creation through decommissioning. Our IT governance structure was comprehensive and effective, yet navigating bureaucratic hurdles, disjointed security approvals, and outdated systems was exhausting.

One particularly challenging area was the VA's GI Bill system, a complex web of legacy applications that were difficult to maintain and modernize.

I was even called to testify before Congress about the system's challenges, highlighting the need for updated technology and streamlined processes. To my surprise, a video clip of my testimony, in which I described the system as complex with an old engine, ended up on *The Daily Show with Trevor Noah*!

While I never expected to find myself on a late-night comedy show, the experience underscored the importance of communicating the complexities of government IT to a wider audience and advocating for the resources needed to modernize these critical systems. To address these challenges, I focused on streamlining processes and implementing Agile methodologies that could deliver faster and more efficient IT solutions.

By utilizing VA's Veteran-Focused Integration Process framework, I integrated Agile methodology into its project management practices and delivered faster and more efficient IT solutions through flexible development cycles and continuous feedback loops.

One of my guiding refrains was, "Put the word *enterprise*

in front of anything VA does, and you will find millions of dollars in savings." I understood that aligning efforts across VA's Administrations and Staff offices had the power to deliver better outcomes for Veterans. Drawing on lessons learned from the Air Force, I adopted a strategic mindset that prioritized goals, collaborative effort, and incremental progress toward lasting impact. The approach was a long game, often requiring "baby steps," but persistence carried the day.

This foundation of enterprise-wide alignment and streamlined processes created the ideal conditions for a fundamental paradigm shift. The move to Software as a Service (SaaS) embodied this evolution, allowing for faster, smarter, and more adaptive solutions that redefined how services were delivered. Building on the groundwork of previous efforts, the SaaS revolution represented not just a new technological direction, but a complete reimagining of what VA could achieve for those it serves.

UNLEASHING THE SAAS REVOLUTION

The largest conference room at VA headquarters buzzed with quiet conversations, its whiteboards still faintly etched with echoes of old ideas. This scene of routine was about to transform. Our mission? To revolutionize how the VA leveraged Software as a Service (SaaS)—a model delivering cloud-based applications via subscription. SaaS promised agility, cost savings, and solutions designed to adapt quickly to the complex needs of Veterans and clinicians alike.

At the session's precise start time—a rarity in VA meetings—a clear voice cut through the room's buzz. The USDS leader—an experienced, determined Gen-Xer—stood confidently, commanding the attention of more than forty VA employees. "Today, we focus on SaaS use cases that deliver real value to Veterans and remove blockers for our frontline clinicians," she stated. Like many who work in VA, her personal connection to the VA's mission was undeniable—her father, a Vietnam combat Veteran affected by Agent Orange, fueled her relentless drive for change. Her words ignited a shift in the room's energy.

I'd initially arrived as an observer, there to validate the shift. But watching the room crackle with purpose, I felt compelled to act. My role was clear. I had to validate this willingness to break from the past. "Tell me more," I said, signaling my endorsement, empowering the team, and opening the way for innovation.

Alongside me, the USDS leader's clarity of vision and personal connection inspired the room, fueling collective determination. Her presence reminded us all why the work mattered so deeply.

What followed was extraordinary. Clinicians, technologists, and analysts collaborated with focus and urgency. Markers flew as bold ideas filled every inch of whiteboard space. Voices surged in collaboration. This was no ordinary brainstorming session. This was momentum at work. The room morphed into a hive of creativity and determination, driven by a shared mission.

I reassured the teams that their bold approach and break from tradition were not just acceptable—they were necessary. By shifting to SaaS, we could accelerate processes that once took over a year to shrink to thirty days or less, embodying the speed, respect, and innovation Veterans deserve. And the SaaS revolution wasn't just about delivering software—it enabled user organizations to make their own choices about whether and how much to invest in automated solutions while offering a better, faster, and cheaper way to deliver improved experiences and outcomes to Veterans.

This was the beginning of the Software as a Service revolution in VA.

THE DEVOPS TRANSFORMATION

By 2018, I took on a pivotal role as Deputy Assistant Secretary for Development and Operations (DevOps), managing nearly half of VA's $4 billion IT budget. More than just a career milestone, this role was a chance to modernize IT systems and, more importantly, deliver meaningful, lasting results for Veterans. To me, DevOps equaled empathy. This was far more than a methodology; it was a philosophy rooted in shared understanding, driven by the belief that every IT decision, whether it involved code, infrastructure, or budget, had a direct impact on the Veteran's experience.

Historically, VA's software developers and operations teams worked in silos, creating inefficiencies and delays. My vision was to break down these walls and foster a culture of communication and mutual respect. Developers needed to understand the challenges faced by the infrastructure operators, who kept their systems running 24/7. Conversely, operations teams needed to appreciate how their infrastructure decisions directly impacted application performance and the experiences of end users, including Veterans and the VA staff serving them. Having worked night shifts in a data center thirty years earlier, I knew firsthand how interconnected these roles truly were.

EMPATHY IN BUDGETING

But the interconnectedness extended beyond team collaboration, reaching even into how we approached budgeting—a process where empathy often got lost. In a year-end budget drill, a spreadsheet can reduce intricate IT systems into lifeless line items, masking the real-world consequences behind each investment decision. What looked like a routine cut to seemingly minor software upgrades might actually mean longer wait times for a Veteran seeking a knee replacement. Saving money by reducing server capacity could delay the processing of Veteran disability claims. Empathy required us to step back from the spreadsheet and consider the people affected by these decisions. We had to prioritize investments that delivered the greatest impact on the end-user experience, recognizing that sometimes "saving" in one area could cost far more in terms of disrupted services and diminished care.

YOU BUILD IT, YOU OWN IT

To foster accountability and empathy, I introduced "You Build It, You Own It" (YBIYOI). This philosophy held everyone responsible for the full life cycle of the systems they created, from development through operation. This principle was rooted in my own experience as a computer operator working the night shift in a data center. Back then, when a program crashed, I had to get the system back up and running, even though I hadn't written the code. While I wrestled with the consequences of their errors, I pictured the programmer sleeping peacefully, dreaming of perfectly executed code. If that were me, I'd want that 2:30 a.m. wake-up call to fix the problem my code had caused. By cultivating shared ownership, we fostered a cultural shift meant to fundamentally change how the teams worked together.

This dedication to empathy extended well beyond internal teams to the Veterans we served every day. I mandated that every IT contract include human-centered design (HCD) principles to ensure our solutions were not only functional but intuitive and tailored to the needs of Veterans and VA staff. Drawing on my experience at the Defense Mapping Agency, I believed that technology existed to serve people—never the other way around. By putting Veterans at the center of everything we did, we strove to build systems that earned trust, inspired ownership, and advanced DevOps beyond a technical approach into a full cultural transformation.

This philosophy proved to be a unifying force connecting the seemingly disparate aspects of IT systems, teams, budgets, and user experience. The work we did had tangible value, not something abstract or theoretical. Every line of code, every infrastructure decision, and every dollar shifted had a ripple effect on the lives of Veterans and the VA staff dedicated to serving them. Empathy was the foundation for meaningful, mission-driven change.

A LEADERSHIP EVOLUTION

These experiences, from navigating SES–political appointee dynamics to driving cultural and operational changes, reflected a larger shift in my own leadership style. Moving from the urgency and precision of DOD to the deliberation and inclusivity of VA required me to reset my mindset. Patience, empathy, and shared commitment emerged as my most effective tools.

The VA presented its own unique set of challenges. Yet, with every hurdle cleared, I saw the impact of our efforts more clearly. Each project, from enterprise transformation to DevOps integration, underscored my commitment to putting Veterans first. And beyond the technical advances, this chapter of my career became a powerful reminder that leadership wasn't about imposing solutions. True leadership was about creating environments where collaboration unlocked outcomes that served a mission far larger than ourselves.

FROM IMPOSSIBLE TO DONE

Under my leadership, the Department of Veterans Affairs began a groundbreaking transformation to move its vast inventory of software applications to a cloud computing infrastructure. Driven by Federal Cloud Smart policies, my team developed a comprehensive cloud strategy that culminated in the 2018 establishment of the Enterprise Cloud Solutions Office and the VA Enterprise Cloud, a secure, multivendor computing environment designed to support Veteran-centric technology solutions.

EARLY CLOUD ADOPTION

In 2017, VA's cloud journey began with a mere ten IT systems, a humble starting point for such a monumental technical and cultural shift. Between 2017 and 2018, my team transitioned over 400,000 email users to Microsoft Office 365, marking the largest federal government adoption of cloud-based email and setting the stage for future initiatives. In 2019, the CIO introduced what seemed like an unattainable goal: migrate 350 applications to the cloud by the end of 2024. However, by 2024, the Office of Information and Technology exceeded this target, migrating over five hundred systems to the cloud. These decisive actions transformed VA into a more agile and responsive IT operation, enabling it to better serve Veterans in ways that were previously unattainable.

MIGRATING THE VETERANS BENEFITS MANAGEMENT SYSTEM

The next very significant milestone was the migration of the Veterans Benefits Management System (VBMS), VA's flagship paperless claims processing system, to the cloud. Migrating VBMS to the cloud was a bold yet nerve-wracking decision, as it was the central, mission-critical application for the Veterans Benefits Administration. Any misstep could have caused the entire VA cloud strategy to collapse. This initiative not only saved $60 million annually but also played a critical role in enhancing the VA's ability to serve Veterans and staff.

The push to migrate VBMS stemmed from performance issues I witnessed in 2017. Several patient-serving applications were plagued by sluggish response times due to computing resource limitations, creating bottlenecks. The cloud's expansive, dynamic computing power offered an appealing solution.

Funding, however, was a challenge. To secure the necessary funding, I had to get creative. I implemented a targeted "tax" on the anticipated IT development budgets for the health and benefits software portfolios. This meant taking a small percentage from each of those projects before their funding was finalized and then pooling those resources to kick-start the cloud migration initiative. Doing so was a calculated risk, temporarily reducing the funds available for those other projects. However, I believed the cloud's benefits—quicker response times for all users and fewer system outages—far outweighed the temporary trade-offs.

The VBMS migration was not without its share of technical complexities, but a strong partnership with the brilliant USDS experts helped navigate these challenges. The team devised a novel phased strategy to physically move huge 100-terabyte chunks of the VBMS database during the day with what amounted to be a super-duper-sized thumb drive, while using VA's own networks to move data at night when network traffic was low.

A CRUCIAL TEST CASE

This strategic approach laid the groundwork for the successful migration of VBMS, which became a crucial test case for cloud adoption within the VA's ecosystem. The stakes were high: VBMS supported up to four thousand users and managed billions of documents, making its cloud migration not only significant but also a litmus test for all future VA computing endeavors.

Despite all the challenges, the migration was completed by April 2019—two months ahead of schedule. The seamless transition inspired confidence across the organization and set the stage for other critical systems to follow suit.

CONQUERING THE "HOLY GRAIL"

Building on VBMS's success, we then tackled the "Holy Grail" of software applications: VA's Electronic Health Record system called "VistA" (Veterans Health Information Systems and Technology Architecture.) VistA was a sprawling, complex ecosystem comprising fifteen million lines of code through nearly two hundred integrated applications accessing petabytes of lab, imaging, and text notes. Dedicated to supporting millions of healthcare clinical, administrative, and financial transactions, it was deemed "impossible" to move to the cloud. Yet, by leveraging the experience gained in earlier migrations, we achieved this milestone. By June 2019, we had migrated the first of VistA's 130 different instantiations, and by 2024, all the VistA instances were successfully migrated to the cloud. What once seemed unattainable had transformed into a defining accomplishment through the power of persistence and innovative thinking.

REAPING THE REWARDS

Through these efforts, the VA reimagined its IT structure. The shift improved service delivery, created a more agile and scalable environment, and provided Veterans with better outcomes. These efforts also underscored fiscal responsibility, showcasing how cloud technologies could meet evolving business needs while exposing actual hosting costs.

One key aspect of this fiscal responsibility was the shift from CapEx (capital expenditures) to OpEx (operating expenditures), a concept I had championed during my time in the private sector. Traditionally, the VA had invested heavily in CapEx, purchasing and maintaining expensive hardware and software infrastructure. This approach often led to large up-front costs and ongoing maintenance expenses. Furthermore, the true cost of services was often obscured, as the expenses associated with capital, inventory, facilities, and government labor were not explicitly tracked or allocated to specific services.

By transitioning to the cloud, the VA was able to move toward an OpEx model, paying for IT services as needed and reducing the burden of owning and managing physical infrastructure. This shift not only provided cost savings but also brought greater transparency and accountability to IT spending. With an OpEx model, the VA knew exactly what it was paying for, as it received a clear invoice for the services consumed. This allowed for better cost management and more informed governance over IT investments.

Throughout my civil service career, a core principle has shaped my approach to effective governance: The government should concentrate on inherently governmental functions while leveraging the private sector's innovation and efficiency where appropriate. This philosophy drove my "Buy Before Build" and "COTS (Commercial Off-the-Shelf) Before Custom" policies, which emphasized procuring ready-made solutions over developing custom ones in-house. By adopting private-sector IT services as needed, the VA could prioritize its core mission of serving Veterans while benefiting from the private sector's agility and expertise. This focus on aligning resources with unique governmental responsibilities has consistently guided my decisions and reinforced my belief in the value of partnership between the public and private sectors.

The successful modernization validated the cloud strategy I led, firmly establishing the VA as a leader in federal IT innovation. On the surface, IT infrastructure modernization—like migrating applications to the cloud—may sound purely technical, and to a large degree it was. But the real impact was far-reaching. The modernized cloud platform provided a flexible computational and data foundation for advanced analytics, innovative artificial intelligence, and machine learning—all of which enabled improved care and services provided to Veterans.

Leading this transformation profoundly shaped me. It deepened my appreciation for the power of collaboration and the single-minded commitment required to drive meaningful change in a large organization. It also reinforced my belief in technology's potential—not just to improve processes, but to transform lives when guided by a purpose greater than itself.

As the VA continues to evolve and embrace new technologies like AI, I am confident it will uncover even more innovative ways to serve those who have served our country. For me, the greatest reward was knowing that my efforts, however small, contributed to a mission that truly matters.

CHAPTER 11

MISSION ACT

THE WEIGHT OF A NATION'S PROMISE

"To care for him who shall have borne the battle and for his widow, and his orphan."

—ABRAHAM LINCOLN

This powerful call to action, etched into the VA's mission, resonated deeply with me as I embarked on one of the most challenging and rewarding chapters of my career. Chapter 11 recounts the implementation of the MISSION Act, a landmark piece of legislation aimed at improving Veterans' access to healthcare. It's a story of perseverance and dedication to fulfilling a promise to those who have sacrificed so much for our country. From navigating bureaucratic hurdles to overcoming technical challenges, this chapter reveals the complexities and triumphs of leading a massive organization through a period of intense transformation.

When	June 2018	2019
Rank	Senior Executive Service	
Location	Dept. of Veterans Affairs (DC)	

THE MISSION ACT

On June 6, 2018, history was made. President Trump signed the MISSION Act into law, carving a bold promise into the VA's mission. This was no ordinary piece of legislation; it was a direct response to the shocking revelations of the 2014 VAMC (Veterans Affairs Medical Center) Phoenix scandal, a dark period that exposed systemic failures within the Phoenix VA Health Care System.

The scandal came to light when whistleblowers revealed troubling practices that had devastating consequences for Veterans. Secret waiting lists were being used to hide the extensive delays in medical care, leaving Veterans to wait months or even years for appointments. Tragically, some saw their conditions worsen, and others lost their lives while waiting for care. To compound the issue, employees were pressured to falsify records, creating the illusion that Veterans were receiving timely treatment. This culture of deception thrived in an environment lacking accountability and oversight, allowing these practices to persist unchecked for years.

The revelations sparked national outrage, igniting a demand for sweeping reform within the VA healthcare system. The MISSION Act emerged as a bold response to this call, embodying a commitment to ensuring Veterans receive the care and respect they deserve. By addressing the systemic issues exposed by the scandal, the Act promised better access to healthcare, greater transparency, and stronger support for caregivers.

With the MISSION Act, dramatic changes were introduced to how Veterans accessed medical care. This legislation expanded their ability to seek treatment from local, non-VA healthcare providers. This was known as "Community Care." It allowed Veterans to seek care in the private sector when wait times for a VA appointment were too long or when VA facilities were too far away.

But lofty promises come with heavy responsibilities. Delivering on the MISSION Act's commitment required the VA to rethink and reengineer its approach to Veteran care. The stakes were even higher with a symbolic deadline for Initial Operating Capability: June 6, 2019, the seventy-fifth anniversary of D-Day. Much like that fateful moment in Normandy, this deadline embodied urgency, transformation, and determination. The comparison wasn't lost on me; this was our opportunity to storm the beaches of entrenched bunkers of bureaucracy and aging infrastructure, delivering a victory for the millions of men and women who had selflessly served their country. More importantly, completing the analysis of the legislation and then, engineering such a complex program in under a year was a "moon shot" for the VA. This endeavor was fraught with challenges, demanding an overhaul of deeply ingrained processes, a very complex technological leap forward, and a cultural shift within the organization. To achieve this feat in such a short timeframe seemed almost impossible, requiring a level of enterprise focus, innovation, and sheer determination that pushed the boundaries of what we thought was possible.

Part of the MISSION Act's implementation relied on a software application called the Decision Support Tool (DST), a deceptively modest but vital piece of software. Its purpose? To guide VA healthcare providers in determining Veterans' eligibility for community care based on the Act's new criteria. But the tool had to work in real time, seamlessly integrating into the VA's sprawling, tangled network of legacy systems. It was like threading a needle while riding a galloping horse.

This was a defining mission for my team, and for me, personally. I knew immediately that this effort would demand every ounce of leadership, resolve, and ingenuity I possessed.

THE CHALLENGE AHEAD

When I took a DST leadership role in January 2019, the clock was already ticking down to D-Day. The MISSION Act had been enacted the previous June, but progress was lagging. DST's design faced significant uncertainty and delays, hampered by incomplete requirements and layers of bureaucratic hurdles. The intricate process of analyzing the legislation, line by line to ensure VA's compliance, only added to the complexity. Compounding these issues were resource shortages, entanglements with legacy VA software applications, and the constant pressure of competing priorities, creating a highly challenging and multifaceted landscape.

And yet, as insurmountable as it seemed, the task carried with it an unmissable sense of urgency. Veterans counting on expanded access to care couldn't afford delays. The June 6, 2019, deadline was more than symbolic; it was carved in stone. The consequences of missing it would ripple through Congress, the media, and most importantly, the lives of those we served.

From the beginning, it was clear that this effort would test me as a leader like nothing before. Every decision had to be calculated, every setback treated as an opportunity to learn and adapt. The risk of failure loomed large, but I viewed this moment as a crucible—a chance to prove what we could accomplish when driven by purpose and galvanized by urgency.

SOLUTIONS AMID CHAOS

The DST's purpose was simple: enable quick and efficient eligibility determinations for the Veterans Community Care Program by automating the MISSION Act criteria. But its creation was anything but simple. Developing the tool required unprecedented collaboration from a wide range of stakeholders, including technologists, clinicians, administrators, and Veterans. Merging these diverse perspectives into a single, cohesive vision was an enormous challenge, but one that brought incredible rewards.

Building the DST was a feat of engineering, coordination, and sheer willpower. Realizing we couldn't rely on traditional planning and development cycles, I turned to Agile and DevOps methodologies—tools ideally suited for navigating tight deadlines and entrenched complexity.

The first step was breaking down the monumental task into manageable pieces. The core principle of Agile—prioritize small, incremental victories, then "Stand on the rock of success, no matter how small"—became our rallying cry. Instead of being paralyzed by the enormity of the project, this approach allowed us to celebrate each step forward, building momentum with every passing week.

But we needed more than incremental Agile software deliveries to succeed. We tore down silos between political appointees, senior leaders, developers, operations teams, and stakeholders, fostering an unprecedented level of collaboration. Daily stand-up meetings at 8:00 a.m. and 5:00 p.m. created a dynamic rhythm where communication flourished, roadblocks vanished, and issues that once lingered for weeks were resolved in mere hours. Our dedication didn't stop at the workweek. Weekend duty was a common commitment, as the entire team pushed relentlessly to maintain momentum. What stood out most to me was the remarkable agency-wide directionality, engagement, and focus—a level of unity I hadn't experienced since witnessing the digital revolution of cartography at the Defense Mapping Agency twenty years earlier. Everyone, from software engineers to frontline clinicians, was united by a shared sense of purpose and accountability.

Key partnerships emerged as the foundation of this effort. Technologists, meticulous in their focus on detail, had to connect with clinicians driven by real-time needs of patient care. While these two groups initially seemed worlds apart, the bridge between them lay in active and empathetic listening, truly understanding each perspective. Engineers came to appreciate the real-world complexities of healthcare, while clinicians gained insight into the capabilities and limits of technology. Over time, their collaboration grew into a shared language rooted in a common mission to improve Veterans' care.

Field staff, administrators, and operations leads also played vital roles. They offered practical insights that grounded the tool in reality. Their input reminded everyone involved that even the smartest technology must adapt to human workflows. Veterans themselves were also indispensable partners. Their feedback and involvement in focus groups ensured that the tool was designed with their needs in mind. They were not passive recipients of care but active contributors to the change we aimed to achieve.

This work also catalyzed a cultural shift within the organization. Like many large institutions, the culture at the outset was siloed, with teams accustomed to working in isolation. But to succeed with the DST, those silos had to come down. This required people from vastly different backgrounds to unite as one team. Breaking down these barriers wasn't easy and demanded vulnerability, admitting when answers weren't clear, and asking for help. It also required trust, which took time to build but became the foundation for progress. Shared successes brought people closer together, and mistakes became learning opportunities.

BREAKING THE BELTWAY BUBBLE

When preparing for the MISSION Act's rollout, we recognized that issuing directives from Washington was not enough. To truly support Veterans and the dedicated teams at VA medical centers, we needed to connect with the people delivering care every day. The Senior Executive Service members of our IT organization embarked on a national emissary mission, fanning out across the country to serve as educators, listeners, and messengers for the MISSION Act. In most cases, they were teamed up with executives from VHA, and many of these teams were stationed at VA Medical Centers on D-Day to witness and support the rollout. By pairing representatives from both the clinical/user perspective and the technical/creator perspective, VA could gain a complete picture of the people, processes, and technology in operation. While our goal was to explain the complexities of the law, we also aimed to learn from the staff on the ground and bring their concerns back to headquarters.

For my part, I chose to visit the Marion VA Medical Center in southern Illinois ahead of D-Day, ensuring I could return to VA headquarters by June 5, the day before the rollout. This visit location was deeply personal for me. I grew up in southern Illinois, a region often referred to as "Little Egypt" for its resemblance to the Nile Delta where the Ohio and Mississippi rivers meet, and returning felt like coming home. The center itself, with its striking pyramid-shaped architecture, was a local landmark that I had driven past often, but this time, I saw it through a new lens—as a part of the VA's mission for which I was responsible.

My visit was nothing short of eye-opening. Coming from the VA's Washington, DC, headquarters, I was used to crafting policies and frameworks at a strategic level, but stepping out of the "DC bubble" and into the field changed my perspective.

The visit reinforced the challenges, complexities, and nuances of the day-to-day experiences of the staff and Veterans that our work at headquarters was meant to support. This was the perfect example of "learning through my fingers." No amount of reports or briefings could have taught me what I learned during those firsthand conversations at Marion.

One interaction stayed with me more than any other. I met a nurse who had been with the VA for over twenty years. As we sat in a small conference room, she shared her concerns in a well-crafted presentation, highlighting the potential challenges of the MISSION Act rollout. She spoke passionately about her dedication to serving Veterans but also expressed her frustration with the limitations she faced. "We're doing our best with what we have," she explained, "but sometimes it feels like we're fighting an uphill battle with outdated technology and bureaucratic hurdles."

After the briefing, I couldn't help but indulge my curiosity. I opened the credenza to peek at the PC that was driving the presentation, and I was stunned by what I saw. Tucked inside was an ancient PC, several generations out of date. In that moment, the weight of my responsibility hit me. This dedicated nurse, tirelessly serving Veterans, was hindered by outdated technology—a stark reminder of the gaps we needed to bridge. I felt a sense of personal failure, a deep regret that I hadn't done more to ensure that proper IT resources reached every corner of the organization.

Overall, I was struck by the sheer dedication and resilience of the healthcare professionals I met there. They faced incredible challenges with grace and tenacity, delivering care to Veterans in ways that inspired awe and respect. That experience made me realize how much I had been missing by not spending more time on the front lines. Listening to their stories, observing their work, and seeing their commitment with my own eyes illuminated the real-world impact of the policies we created. This powerful reminder emphasized that leadership meant connecting with those on the ground, understanding their needs, and empowering them to succeed.

THE JOINT OPERATIONS CENTER TRANSFORMATION

To prepare for the MISSION Act's rollout on June 6, we adopted the mindset of "Train like we fight." This military-inspired approach meant creating intense, near-real practice drills under pressure to ensure readiness. We set up VHA's Healthcare Operations Center like a wartime Crisis Action Team Joint Operations Center (modeled after my Desert Shield experience at USTRANSCOM), complete with a digital wall of dashboards and a physical command presence in the room.

The JOC was the nerve center for the operation, where real-time data fed decisions and allowed us to remain agile. Establishing this physical hub epitomized what made the DST project different from so many others. This setup brought disciplined trouble-ticketing principles to life, combining situational awareness, rapid communication, and adaptive problem-solving under one roof. For the first time, software product managers (PMs) were put on call status, forcing a shift to the Product Line Management philosophy and reinforcing the YBIYOI mindset.

The creation of the JOC was a game-changer, as unlike DOD, the VA did not normally function as an operational entity. This physical hub of activity became the nerve center of the MISSION Act's rollout. Physicians, IT professionals, and business champions worked shoulder to shoulder, tackling challenges in real time. The JOC was about unifying two disparate cultures under a single mission, getting everybody "in the room" and reducing friction by making quick, clear decisions.

The cultural evolution that followed was profoundly inspiring. An organization once fragmented began to resemble a cohesive ecosystem. Trust allowed teams to innovate, adapt, and pivot when challenges arose. The process wasn't without its frustrations, but the shared commitment to and clarity of the mission—supporting our nation's Veterans—kept everyone aligned. Slowly, a team of individuals became a community united by purpose.

One of the most important roles to emerge from this collaboration was that of the "business champion," a bridge builder between OIT and VHA, responsible for aligning priorities and ensuring the voices of end users were heard throughout development. More than an advocate, the business champion facilitated open channels of communication and trust. He translated the practical concerns and feedback of VHA staff into actionable insights for IT development teams while demystifying technical constraints or processes for end users. This role minimized misunderstandings, managed user expectations, aligned goals, and kept the focus on delivering tools and services to improve the lives of Veterans, caregivers, and VA staff. By fostering dialogue and building trust between clinicians and developers, the business champion played an indispensable role in our success.

SILENCING THE "GOOD IDEA FAIRY"

Our progress faced challenges, particularly from the "good idea fairy," which symbolized well-meaning but poorly timed suggestions. While these ideas were well-intentioned, during the crucial MISSION Act period, they risked causing more harm than good by introducing unnecessary distractions, leading to scope creep and creating friction within our teams. To mitigate this, we established a clear process for managing these "good ideas." We documented each suggestion, creating a backlog of potential features and enhancements for future consideration. This not only acknowledged the value of these ideas but also ensured that clinicians and other stakeholders could see that their input was being taken seriously. However, we also had to be firm in prioritizing the immediate needs of the MISSION Act implementation.

Growing up with my father's playful stories of "mischievous gremlins" that inhabited everyday objects, I learned to see life's little frustrations as opportunities to pause, recalibrate, and defeat them through perseverance. This lesson turned out to be the very tool I needed to silence the "good idea fairy." Much like the gremlins, the fairy disrupted progress, but instead of frustrations, it dangled shiny new ideas that tugged at your focus. Dealing with gremlins taught me that patient discipline was essential, and the same rule applied when the fairy flew in with suggestions that sounded good but weren't urgent.

To combat this, we adopted a simple mantra during our daily management scrums: "Not no, but not now." This phrase ensured that promising but nonessential ideas were noted and deferred, allowing us to maintain laser focus on immediate priorities. Achieving this required discipline and a shared commitment to the finish line.

POLITICAL CROSSWINDS AND A USDS BOMBSHELL

By early March 2019, we were starting to feel assured about our trajectory. Then, out of nowhere, an internal USDS report dropped like a bombshell, shattering our momentum and causing an abrupt upheaval.

Leaked to the media, the report raised serious doubts about DST, warning that the tool's design could disrupt clinicians' day-to-day workflows, and recommending a complete overhaul—an impossible proposition a mere three months away from the deadline. I was shocked and disappointed.

The timing of the leak, just three months before June 6, couldn't have been worse. Although the report had the trappings of a technical assessment, its political ramifications represented something much more sinister. Members of the VA's political leadership viewed the report as a deliberate attempt by USDS, an entity born during the Obama administration, to undermine a key Veterans policy achievement by President Trump.

I vividly remember being in the VA CIO's large conference room during a highly charged meeting where USDS leadership was under heavy scrutiny for their actions. Tensions peaked when they shockingly implied that VA physicians "were not real doctors." While they denied any intent to insult or oppose, it was clear to me at that point that their focus had strayed from the realm of technology and had instead become entangled with political agenda.

That moment marked a turning point for me. USDS's dazzling brilliance I so admired was tarnished and dulled by the shadow of politics. Their actions crossed a line of acceptability, breaching a fundamental principle of the federal career civil service: to remain politically neutral while still being accountable to democratically elected leaders. In my view, the actions of USDS's leadership, whether intentional or not, had undermined this principle. By allowing their technical assessment to become entangled with the perception of political motivations, they had compromised the integrity of the process and eroded the trust that is essential for effective public service.

Determined not to derail our mission, we chose to continue

forward with the original DST design. It wasn't perfect, but we would deliver on schedule, securing an important victory for private sector choice in Veterans' healthcare.

A PROMISE AND A CRISIS

The clock in the Joint Operations Center seemed to tick louder the closer it got to midnight. June 6 was just around the corner, and with it came the weight of a promise—a commitment to launch the MISSION Act on a day of deep historical significance. Every contingency had been planned for, every detail scrutinized. Yet, in the final hour, the unexpected struck.

At 11:30 p.m. on June 5, a chilling message crackled through the tense silence. The IT team, applying what they thought were final software patches, had instead unleashed chaos. Their latest changes hadn't just introduced a flaw. They had broken the DST system entirely. The technical heart of the MISSION Act's implementation was now a ticking time bomb, threatening to derail everything we had worked for. The air in the room seemed to sharpen, tension snapping into place like the click of a taut wire. Panic was a shape you could suddenly feel in the room.

ON THE PRECIPICE

My mind raced, grappling with the implications. We had a backup plan—a manual process to keep operations running if the system failed—but that wasn't the story we wanted to tell on a day that would set the tone for the future of Veteran care. Our IT team, tired and grim-faced, stood in the eye of the storm, knowing all eyes were on us.

And then the shift began. The echoes of old antagonisms

stirred, creeping into the room like whispers from a shadowy corner. Fingers poised, ready to point. Positions were fortified, ready to defend. Our IT team, drained and demoralized, stood in quiet anticipation of the inevitable backlash. We were teetering on the edge of a familiar precipice, watching the toxic choice of "business success or IT failure" beginning to rear its ugly head once again.

To me, this threatened the launch of the MISSION Act, the delicate connections we had built as a team, and the shared spirit we had worked so hard to nurture. A moment like this could unravel trust and fracture us in ways that would take far more than time to repair.

A LEADER'S RESOLVE

Tension filled the room as IT leaders bent over laptops, clinicians conferred in tight circles, and commands bounced back and forth. The urgency was palpable, every second feeling like an hour.

And then, it happened.

Our VHA business champion, a respected MD, weighed in and rose to the moment, not with a message of anger or blame, but with something far more powerful. He could have thrown the IT team under the bus. He could have taken a page out of the old "us versus them" playbook. It would have been the simpler, more predictable path. It would have been easy, even expected. But instead, he chose a different path, one of unity and resolve.

His decision was shared with the room. "Roll back. Use the previous version." It was less than ideal, and less than we had hoped for, but it was a plan. A path forward. No hesitation, no fingers pointed, just a course of action to keep the mission alive.

Ironically, it wasn't so much the technical reset that shifted the momentum; it was the underlying message. This wasn't about individual failures. This was about collective strength.

THE ROLLBACK

The transformation in the room was palpable. Once frozen with the weight of the problem, we now sprang into action with newfound determination. The IT team in the JOC, with fingers on keyboards and phones to our ears, relayed the decision to the software teams, restoring the previous version with precision born of expertise and trust. Clinicians jumped in with contingency plans to keep operations steady no matter what. The room, once fracturing under stress, had coalesced into a single, unstoppable force.

Time twisted and stretched as we raced against the clock, fingers a blur across keyboards, voices sharp and focused. Midnight loomed, each second a hammer blow against the silence. And then, success. The rollback was complete. The system was stable. DST was operational. A wave of relief washed over the room, a shared exhale of "*We* did it, the *entire* VA, *together*."

A DEFINING VICTORY

Midnight passed, marking the launch of the MISSION Act—on time, intact, and under the watchful eyes of a nation.

Yet the memory that remains with me isn't just the relief of averting a system disaster. What stays with me was something far deeper and more meaningful. We had faced a storm that could have torn us apart, but instead, it brought us closer. We had stared into the abyss of failure, but instead of fracturing, we had become something stronger, something more resilient.

The instinct to blame, to divide, had been overcome by a shared commitment to the mission and to each other. The spirit of "us," fueled by one leader's refusal to yield to division, had prevailed.

That night, we achieved more than launching the MISSION Act successfully. Together, we redefined what it meant to be a team at the VA. I left that room with a profound understanding: our strength lay in our unity, and as long as we stood together, no obstacle was insurmountable.

The Decision Support Tool represented a microcosm of the transformation needed across the VA. It showed that government agencies could innovate with pace and purpose without losing sight of their core mission. For me, DST was a defining chapter in my career that offered a lasting lesson on the power of purpose-driven collaboration.

JUNE 6, 2019: TRIUMPH ON D-DAY

June 6, 2019, marked a pivotal moment with the implementation of the MISSION Act and the Decision Support Tool. Yet, this project was never just about a piece of software; it represented something far bigger. The DST was a small but vital component of the vast and intricate Veterans health ecosystem. Its true significance lay not in technology itself but in the collective effort, partnerships, and cultural transformation that fueled its creation and implementation.

Reflecting on that experience, several lessons stood out. First, collaboration was essential, but it proved to be an art that required patience, humility, and commitment. Without it, even the best technology had the potential to fail. With it, something as seemingly small as the DST became a powerful catalyst for change.

Second, partnerships were most impactful when they crossed traditional boundaries. Listening to voices outside the usual circles—whether field staff, administrators, or even critics—strengthened the project. Innovation thrived when diverse perspectives were respected and incorporated. Taking the time to understand and value the contributions of all stakeholders made the end result significantly stronger.

Finally, cultural change was more about people than processes or technology. Organizations often focused on tools, but the real transformation happened when trust, respect, and shared purpose took root. None of what was achieved with the DST would have been possible without thousands of individuals contributing in their own ways. Their collective effort became the true legacy of the project.

Looking back, June 6, 2019, holds a special place in my memory. The tool itself was a small rock of success upon which I stood, but the teams that built it were the boulders that made me proud. The DST was a symbol of our shared commitment to serving Veterans better. In addition to being a technical accomplishment, it proved what's possible when we dare to collaborate, listen, and evolve together.

A WELL-EARNED VICTORY

The successful implementation of the MISSION Act in June 2019 was more than just the culmination of one project—it was the apex of my career. For months, we had fought in the trenches together, shoulder to shoulder, against overt challenges and unseen pressures. That June milestone represented a hard-won victory for the teams who labored tirelessly and for Veterans. There was a palpable sense of triumph as I watched our work transform from long, grueling days into a tangible, meaningful legacy. The echoes of that success filled me with pride but also nudged me toward deeper reflection.

Looking back on the successful implementation of the MISSION Act, I am struck by the extraordinary enterprise-wide unity that propelled our efforts. This remarkable alignment wasn't accidental; it stemmed from deliberate and effective management actions by our CIO, a former Marine, who embodied the core values of judgment and decisiveness. The MISSION Act was a case study in executive government management, showcasing how prioritizing a single initiative above all else galvanized a massive organization. For the first time, the OIT team, government civilians and contractors alike, rallied with an "all hands on deck" mindset, channeling their energy into learning the intricacies of the Act, addressing challenges with urgency, and driving its success. The result was a level of dedication and focus I hadn't witnessed since I was part of the digital revolution of cartography at the Defense Mapping Agency twenty years earlier. This served as a profound reminder that strong leadership, shared values, clear communication, and collective effort can overcome immense challenges and achieve extraordinary outcomes.

By the time September 2019 arrived, and I officially ushered in my sixty-fifth birthday, I could feel the weight of a lifetime's worth of contributions settling around me. I thought about the early days of my career, filled with youthful ambition, and how each moment, each struggle, and every hard-earned lesson had prepared me for the final crescendo of delivering the MISSION Act. Turning sixty-five felt symbolic, not of slowing down, but of reaching the summit after an arduous yet immensely rewarding climb.

With each passing day after that September birthday, I began to see it more clearly—the end of this chapter and the start of something new. The halls where I spent years problem-solving, innovating, and collaborating held memories that I knew would stay etched in my heart. The faces of colleagues, who had become like family, demonstrated the power of shared purpose and the strength of human connection. My decision to retire in December 2019 came not from weariness but from a profound sense of fulfillment. The fight had been worth it, and every ounce of effort had led to this crescendo.

December's chill mirrored the bittersweet end of my career, a fulfilling journey that had given me everything I dared to dream of and more. With each farewell, I felt a rush of nostalgia, a bittersweet mix of gratitude and longing. And yet, there was peace in knowing that the work we had done would continue to ripple outward, improving lives and shaping a better future. This moment did not mark the end of my story but the start of something I had earned—time for reflection, renewal, and perhaps, a pathway back to a quieter kind of purpose. The road behind me was long and winding, filled with trials and triumphs, but it had led me precisely where I was meant to be.

CHAPTER 12

A FULL CIRCLE OF PURPOSE

"What you leave behind is not what is engraved in stone monuments, but what is woven into the lives of others."

—PERICLES

This quote from Pericles speaks to the heart of what I hope to convey in this memoir. It's not just about the milestones I achieved or the positions I held, but about the impact I had on the missions I served. It's about the relationships I built, the challenges we overcame together, and the legacy of service that I hope to leave behind. This conclusion reflects on the lessons I learned throughout my career, the values that guided my journey, and the importance of finding purpose and making a difference in the world.

A CAREER IN PERSPECTIVE

Can a life dedicated to public service truly make a difference? Can you find meaning and purpose within the complexities and frustrations of government bureaucracy? This personal story also serves as a reflection on the essence of dedicating oneself to public service, embracing challenges, and finding meaning in complex responsibilities. The narrative highlights the quiet satisfaction that comes from knowing your work holds value, even when unrecognized or unseen. And it's about the legacy we leave behind in the lives we touch and the systems we improve.

But it's also about something more. Throughout these pages, I've aimed to inspire and guide you to find purpose and make a difference through a life dedicated to service. Whether you're a seasoned civil servant or just starting your career, or you are simply seeking a more meaningful path, my hope is that this book has illuminated the possibilities.

Over the course of this book, we've examined that mission from a variety of angles—through moments of individual growth, organizational transformation, and national importance. I hope, above all, that it's shown you how purpose underpins even the most frustrating parts of civil service. From serving those who wear the uniform to those who benefit from the countless invisible functions of government, service is an unbroken thread.

Now, as we close this memoir, I'll share the culmination of what I've learned—the tenets that shaped my career and the lessons I hope will inspire yours.

Reflecting on the milestones and roadblocks of my civil service career brings a sense of humility. Frustrations come to mind easily—bureaucratic red tape, challenges posed by hierarchical structures, and the overwhelming inertia of outdated systems. These were constant companions, often testing my patience and resolve. But looking back, I realize these struggles weren't in vain. They were the forge that shaped my understanding of leadership, resilience, and the importance of being driven by a mission.

LEADING THROUGH CHANGE

My leadership style has been as much a journey of transformation as my career itself. In the early years, I was driven by a desire for efficiency and precision. I focused on achieving measurable results, making quick decisions, and following established processes. This approach served me well in technical roles and project management positions, where clear objectives and deadlines were paramount.

However, as I took on more complex challenges and leadership responsibilities, I began to recognize the limitations of this approach. I realized that true leadership was about empowering others, building consensus, and fostering a shared sense of purpose. This realization led me to embrace a more collaborative and empathetic style, where I prioritized relationships, encouraged open communication, and sought to understand diverse perspectives.

This shift wasn't always easy. I had to push myself beyond my comfort zone, openly acknowledge moments when I lacked all the answers, and place trust in the combined knowledge and expertise of my team. But ultimately, it proved to be the most rewarding aspect of my leadership journey. By embracing vulnerability and fostering a culture of collaboration, I was able to achieve far greater results than I could have ever imagined. This shift in perspective also mirrored a deeper transformation in how I viewed the value of my work. The focus shifted away from personal gain or recognition, centering instead on the positive impact made on other people's lives and the shared mission we were dedicated to serving. Whether it was supporting our nation's military through technology or streamlining benefits and healthcare for veterans, I found greater fulfillment in contributing to something larger than myself.

THE ESSENCE OF LEADERSHIP

Leadership, I discovered, goes beyond exercising authority. True leadership involves fostering an environment where individuals feel empowered to thrive, explore new ideas, and achieve success. Whether I was managing a team of IT specialists or aligning cross-agency policies, the aim was always to empower others with a shared sense of purpose. This is a core principle that I hope this book has conveyed. You don't have to be at the top to lead, and position alone doesn't create impact. What moves the mission forward are the values that guide you and your ability to connect those values with action.

From my earliest roles to overseeing transformational initiatives like the MISSION Act, the significance of collaboration became glaringly evident. No mission in civil service, or perhaps anywhere, thrives in isolation. Take, for example, the development of the Decision Support Tool for the MISSION Act. What seemed like an insurmountable challenge showcased the power of teamwork. Technologists and clinicians, once operating in separate worlds, came together, bridging the gap between their distinct perspectives to create a solution that ultimately improved the lives of veterans. This kind of collaboration, where individuals with diverse skills and backgrounds unite around a shared purpose, is what fuels true progress.

THE POWER OF PERSEVERANCE

Finally, I'm reminded of the importance of perseverance. Every victory, every milestone achieved, was preceded by moments of doubt, frustration, and the temptation to give up. But when I felt like I couldn't push forward any longer, I'd remember those words from my grandmother, "You're like a train on a track. No matter the obstacles, if you stay the course, you'll reach your destination." The belief in the power of persistence and the strength of mission-driven teamwork grounded me during moments of chaos. The perspective stemmed not from naive optimism but from trust in the process and unflagging determination to move forward.

LEADING AT THE TOP

Reaching the Senior Executive Service was a milestone, but also an accomplishment that brought unique challenges. The SES is a demanding world that requires expertise and political savvy, the ability to navigate complex stakeholder relationships, and a deep understanding of how to drive change within large organizations. It's a role where decisions have far-reaching implications, and the pressure to deliver results is immense. But it's also incredibly rewarding. You have the opportunity to shape policies, influence programs, and make a real difference in the lives of the people you serve.

One of the most valuable lessons I learned in the SES was the importance of building consensus. You can't lead effectively in isolation. You need to be able to bring people together, forge alliances, and create buy-in for your vision. This requires strong communication skills, empathy, and a willingness to compromise.

The SES also taught me the value of mentorship. Throughout my career, I benefited from the guidance and support of mentors who helped me navigate challenges, develop my skills, and reach my full potential. From my first supervisor, who patiently showed me the ropes as a GS-1 clerk, to my DMA mentor, who fostered my passion for programming and innovation, to the Colonel at USTRANSCOM who taught me the difference between "RPM and MPH," each one left an indelible mark. They not only imparted knowledge and skills but also instilled confidence and a belief in my abilities.

Mentorship is a two-way street. As I progressed in my career, I had the opportunity to mentor others, sharing my experiences and insights to help them navigate their own paths. Mentorship is an investment in the future, a way to pass on the torch of knowledge, experience, and passion to the next generation of leaders.

FORTUNE FAVORS THE PREPARED

Reflecting on my journey, I see how fortune greatly influenced my path. However, timing and good luck alone could not dictate the outcome. Success came from my readiness to face challenges head-on, my commitment to learning and personal growth, and my ability to take calculated risks, which enabled me to seize opportunities as they emerged. As Louis Pasteur famously said, "Chance favors the prepared mind."

Throughout my life, I've found that fortune often appears in disguise. It might have been a chance encounter in a hallway, a newspaper at the checkout counter, or a seemingly insignificant piece of information that sparks a new idea or opens a new door. But if you're not prepared—if you haven't honed your skills, cultivated your network, and nurtured your curiosity—those opportunities might pass you by.

From my early days as a GS-1 clerk, I sought out challenges, learned new technologies, and built relationships with colleagues and mentors. This foundation allowed me to seize opportunities when they arose, whether it was digital cartography at DMA, leading critical IT initiatives at USTRANSCOM, or driving cloud transformation at VA.

Of course, there were times when fortune didn't seem to be

on my side. I faced setbacks, disappointments, and moments of self-doubt. But even in those challenging times, my preparedness, my skills, my knowledge, and my commitment to service helped me to navigate those obstacles and emerge stronger.

The lesson is clear: While we can't always control the circumstances we find ourselves in, we can control how we prepare for them. By cultivating our skills, building relationships, and staying open to new possibilities, we can increase our chances of encountering fortune and create a path toward a more fulfilling and impactful life.

So, to those who seek to make a difference, I offer this advice: Be prepared. Hone your skills, nurture your curiosity, and build a network of support. And when fortune smiles upon you, be bold enough to seize the moment and embrace the opportunities that come your way. For it is in those accidental moments of serendipity, where preparation meets opportunity, that we often find our greatest successes and discover our true potential.

TYING LESSONS TO THE CORE PRINCIPLE

This brings us back to the heart of the book. The question wasn't just whether being "good enough for government work" was good enough for me. The broader question—one I didn't know I was asking until much later—was whether it could be good enough for the people we serve.

The core principle of this memoir is that public service is worth it, but it's only as good as the care, leadership, and innovation you're willing to bring into your role. Civil service, particularly in mission-oriented environments like defense and veterans' welfare, involves more than adhering to rules or finishing assignments. The true purpose lies in creating meaningful solutions that advance the mission and genuinely impact people's lives, even when systemic obstacles stand in the way. It's about seeing the humanity behind process charts and remembering that every policy, every line of code, every budget executed has ripple effects far beyond the conference room.

A CALL TO ACTION

Now, it's your turn. Take these lessons, these stories, and make them your own. Whether you're a seasoned civil servant, a budding entrepreneur, or simply someone seeking a more meaningful path, the message is the same: Find your purpose and embrace the challenges that come with it.

For my fellow civil servants, remember that the work you do matters. You are the ones who keep the wheels turning, the systems running, and the mission moving forward. You are the ones who make a difference in the lives of others, even when it's unseen or unappreciated. Embrace the challenge, for within it lies the opportunity to meet high standards and to set them. Be prepared to accomplish great things, to innovate, to lead, and to leave your mark on the world. Strive to make a positive impact, even when faced with limitations and setbacks. Know that your dedication and commitment to service matter, regardless of the outcome. And you are the ones who will leave a legacy of service that will inspire generations to come.

This call to action extends beyond those in government. The appeal is for anyone striving to create meaningful change. No matter your field, ground yourself in purpose. Find your "why" and let it guide your actions. Collaborate within your organization and beyond. Embrace lifelong learning and pursue excellence relentlessly. Never give up on your goals, no matter how challenging they may seem.

The lessons of collaboration, perseverance, and leadership are universal. By applying them to your own endeavors, you can unlock new levels of fulfillment and create a ripple effect of positive change that extends far beyond your immediate sphere.

There's a bond between us now. You're no longer just a reader, and I'm no longer just the writer. We are colleagues united by shared values. Together, in whatever role we perform, we can do more, lift others higher, and leave the systems we work in better than we found them.

THE FIRST AND LAST QUESTION

Looking back over fifty years to that summer I spent as a GS-1 clerk at Scott Air Force Base, I can now answer the question I asked back then: "Was being 'good enough for government work' going to be good enough for me?" It's a question that has echoed through the decades, a constant reminder of the low bar often assumed by those who misunderstand the true meaning of public service. But it was more than just a question about a career; it was a question about my values. Could I be satisfied in an environment where doing the bare minimum was acceptable? Could I work alongside people who didn't share my sense of responsibility and commitment to doing their best?

Here's what I've learned over these years: Public service is not about "good enough." It's about doing work that matters, work that has the potential to affect the lives of others in meaningful ways. It's about working toward a mission greater than yourself. The "good enough" cliché was a misrepresentation of the dedication and perseverance I witnessed throughout my career. The standard I saw was high, because that was the standard our citizens and veterans deserved and the standard I set for myself.

BEYOND "GOOD ENOUGH"

Looking back, I recognize that the question of "good enough" was never about meeting someone else's standards. For me, it was always about setting my own goals—pushing myself to doing the best I could with what I had and refusing to settle for less than what the mission demanded. Was I good enough for government work? Did I meet the challenge? Did I deliver on the promise of service?

I believe the answer is yes. Not because I never faltered. I did. There were times when the obstacles seemed insurmountable, the resources scarce, and the systems overwhelming. But my work was grounded in the belief that the mission was worth it, that the people we served—veterans, service members, and citizens—deserved every ounce of effort I could give.

It was never about being perfect or extraordinary. It was about making a difference, even a small difference, where and when it mattered. It was about striving to create positive outcomes, even when the road was difficult. And it was about knowing that my efforts contributed to something beyond myself—a mission that gave my career meaning and my life purpose.

And that, I can say without hesitation, is where I found purpose in public service.

CHAPTER 13 (SUPPLEMENT)

CLIMBING THE LADDER

A GUIDE TO THE SENIOR EXECUTIVE SERVICE

"Always bear in mind that your own resolution to succeed is more important than any other one thing."

—ABRAHAM LINCOLN

This quote underscores the critical role of inner drive and determination in achieving this challenging goal. The path to the SES is not easy; it requires overcoming obstacles, navigating setbacks, and maintaining unswerving dedication. Lincoln's words serve as a powerful reminder that one's own resolve and commitment to the goal are paramount in overcoming these challenges and ultimately reaching the desired destination. While external factors like mentorship, networking, and timing are important, it is one's inner strength and belief in their own potential that will ultimately determine their success in reaching the highest levels of public service.

FROM ASPIRATION TO ACTION

Have you dreamed of leading at the highest levels of government, of making decisions that shape policies and impact millions of lives? This supplement is for those who aspire to achieve the highest levels of public service—those who dream of leading with impact and leaving a lasting legacy. Whether you're new to your federal career or a seasoned professional ready for the next chapter, this guide will help you prepare for the challenges and opportunities of the Senior Executive Service (SES).

The SES role is a mission requiring resilience, strategic thinking, and a strong commitment to the greater good. This guide distills lessons from my own path to the SES into practical steps, equipping you to thrive, not just survive, in the realm of executive leadership. Along the way, I'll demystify the realities of the SES, address misconceptions, and map out a course for you to achieve your goals.

For me, success in the SES was never about titles or prestige. It was about making a difference—shaping policy, driving innovation, and opening doors for others. It was and still is about creating something meaningful that stands the test of time. If you share that vision, this guide can help you prepare for the climb and embrace the opportunities that come with it.

DEMYSTIFYING THE SES

When I first envisioned the SES, I pictured prestige, stability, and the power to create monumental change. But as I stepped closer to this summit, those misconceptions dissolved, replaced by lessons about the true meaning of leadership.

THE SES IS ABOUT SERVICE, NOT STATUS

Leadership in the SES does not revolve around exercising unlimited power. True leadership focuses on advancing a mission while navigating the limitations of a larger system. I learned this firsthand at the VA when a carefully crafted proposal of mine was derailed by political dynamics beyond my control. It was a reminder that leadership at this level demands humility and resilience, not control.

COMPENSATION ISN'T THE REWARD

Initially, I was enticed by the financial rewards associated with the SES. But over time, I realized true fulfillment came from influencing policy, driving innovation, and creating a lasting positive impact, rather than chasing dollars and cents.

STABILITY IS NOT GUARANTEED

Climbing higher on the career ladder often means more uncertain footing. Budget cuts, political shifts, and organizational restructuring are inevitable in the SES. But I found that the greatest stability came not from external circumstances but from within—when I was contributing most earnestly from the heart. Dispelling these illusions reshaped my understanding of leadership. Once the romanticized images fell away, I came to appreciate the SES as a crucible for resilience and growth.

FIFTEEN STEPS TO BECOMING AN SES

Understanding the realities of the SES is just the beginning. To prepare for this demanding and rewarding role, you need a clear plan of action. Drawing from my own experiences and lessons learned, I've outlined fifteen actionable steps to help you stand out, overcome obstacles, and thrive in this demanding and rewarding role.

1. MASTER THE EXECUTIVE CORE QUALIFICATIONS

The Executive Core Qualifications (ECQs), Leading Change, Leading People, Results Driven, Business Acumen, and Building Coalitions, are essential to thriving in executive leadership. Each represents a critical competency designed to drive organizational success while fostering innovation, accountability, and collaboration.

Adapting to the Evolving Landscape of Leadership

The ECQs themselves have evolved since I first began my journey to the SES. In recognition of the changing demands of leadership in the twenty-first century, the Office of Personnel Management updated the ECQs in 2025, with a greater emphasis on strategic thinking, innovation, and the ability to navigate a complex and rapidly changing environment.

Here are some of the key changes in the new ECQs and how they reflect the skills and experiences I've developed throughout my career:

Leading Change: The new ECQs retain the original focus on bringing about strategic change but now include data literacy and systems thinking as subcompetencies. This aligns with my experience using data to drive decision-making and innovation, such as developing the CTRS at USTRANSCOM and leading the VA's cloud transformation initiatives. It also reflects my understanding of how different systems within organizations interact and my ability to lead change holistically.

Leading People: This ECQ now explicitly includes interpersonal skills and building workplace culture as subcompetencies. This resonates with my efforts to foster collaboration, build trust, and create inclusive environments where everyone feels valued and empowered to contribute. It also reflects my commitment to mentoring, coaching, and supporting the development of my team members.

Results Driven: This ECQ remains largely the same but emphasizes strategic communication more explicitly, particularly in broad agency-wide changes such as the MISSION Act in VA. This aligns with my experience using communication to achieve goals, build consensus, and inspire action. It also reflects my ability to tailor my communication style to different audiences and use storytelling to convey complex information effectively.

Business Acumen: This ECQ now encompasses leveraging technology to drive innovation and efficiency, instead of just "technology management." This reflects my passion for using technology to improve processes and achieve better outcomes. It also aligns with my experience implementing cloud solutions, championing Agile and DevOps methodologies, and advocating for the adoption of new technologies to modernize government IT systems.

Building Coalitions: This ECQ continues to focus on coalition-building but with a stronger emphasis on interagency and interdepartmental collaboration. This reflects my experience working across different agencies and departments to achieve common goals, such as my involvement in the DPS modernization effort at DMA and the MISSION Act implementation at the VA. It also highlights my ability to build partnerships, navigate organizational complexities, and foster a shared sense of purpose among diverse stakeholders.

Here's how I developed and demonstrated the required ECQ skills:

A. Leading Change

- **Thesis:** Leading Change means driving strategic transformation by creating and implementing a vision in a dynamic environment. Effective leadership embraces change, guiding others with vision and determination, though success often comes through learning from missteps. But I'll admit, I didn't always get it right the first time.
- **Example:** At DMA, I spearheaded a project to replace the outdated system of transporting magnetic data tapes with a secure digital network, a bold initiative I called "Trucks Suck," to capture both the humor and the urgency of eliminating the physical shipment of magnetic tapes between map production facilities. At first, I underestimated just how deeply people were attached to the old ways. I thought the benefits of modernization would speak for themselves, but I quickly learned that change was as much about emotion as it was about logic. I faced pushback, skepticism, and even outright refusal to change. Then, I had to take a step back and really listen to people's concerns, something I wasn't naturally good at in the beginning. It was humbling to realize that my enthusiasm for what I thought was a good idea wasn't enough. I needed to build trust with stakeholders involved in the old processes. Slowly, through dialogue and persistence, I was able to gain support for an electronic rather than a digital exchange of data. That experience demonstrated that leading change relied on patience and clear communication rather than assuming a good idea would naturally attract support through its logic and appeal.

B. Leading People

- **Thesis:** Effective leadership involves fostering collaboration, teamwork, and conflict resolution, creating an environment that supports employee development and aligns with the organization's mission, vision, and goals. Truly understanding and addressing the personal concerns of a team is central to this effort. This was a lesson I learned firsthand during a challenging period at DMAAC.
- **Example:** During the shift to digital map production, potential layoffs cast a heavy shadow over the team. The fears were deeply personal for many, as friends, acquaintances, and even family members were at risk of losing their jobs. Initially, I focused on efficiency and solutions, failing to grasp the emotional gravity of the situation. This approach left my team feeling disconnected and mistrustful.

Taking the time to listen to their concerns revealed just how personal the fears really were. Admitting that I had overlooked this aspect opened the door to rebuilding trust. Through honest conversations and collaborative efforts, I addressed their anxieties while keeping the team aligned with the goals of the transition. That experience reinforced the importance of empathy and connection in guiding a team through their toughest moments.

C. Results Driven

- **Thesis:** Achieving meaningful results requires focusing on goals, meeting customer needs, and using expertise, risk assessment, and data to drive optimal decisions. By enhancing the accuracy and quality of product distribution, I successfully met a critical organizational need while fulfilling customer requirements.

- **Example:** I have always been a results-oriented person, though I've learned that success often comes with challenges and lessons along the way. At DMA, I had the opportunity to contribute to the development of the Image Manipulation Station (IMS), a system designed to help analysts validate and modify terrain elevation data in real time. While I'm proud of the role I played, the process wasn't without its hurdles. There were many moments of uncertainty and trial and error as I worked to refine the system. Ultimately, this innovation improved the accuracy and efficiency of the mapmaking process, reducing product distribution errors and ensuring critical information reached the Air Force on time. By staying focused on the needs of the end user and collaborating with my mentor to overcome obstacles, I was able to demonstrate the value of a results-driven approach and contribute meaningfully to the agency's mission success.

D. Business Acumen

- **Thesis:** Business acumen requires the ability to strategically manage human, financial, and information resources to drive organizational success. By aligning financial, technical, and personnel assets effectively, I approached resource stewardship as an opportunity to drive mission impact.
- **Example:** Business acumen means connecting resources to outcomes in a way that drives organizational success. When developing the Civilian Training Requirements System (CTRS) at USTRANSCOM, I initially faced significant challenges. Not only were budgets and financial strategies unfamiliar territory, but the makeup of the command's civilian personnel system was also unknown to me. I had to dissect its structure and data in order to feed the anal-

yses calculated by CTRS. Through persistence and a clear vision, I designed the CTRS to demonstrate how targeted training investments directly enhanced mission readiness. By using the command's own data to link resources with measurable outcomes, I reshaped perceptions of civilian training programs, shifting the view from training costs to civilians' skills as indispensable strategic assets. This successful reframing not only defended critical funding but also ensured that financial decisions were aligned with the organization's mission and long-term objectives.

The development of the CTRS reinforced a key lesson about business acumen—success relies less on being a subject matter expert and more on staying focused on connecting resources to meaningful outcomes.

E. Building Coalitions

- **Thesis:** Building coalitions involves fostering collaboration, bridging divides, and creating an environment where diverse stakeholders with different, sometimes opposing, interests feel heard, valued, and aligned toward a shared purpose, enabling stronger relationships and meaningful outcomes.
- **Example:** Building coalitions is about fostering a shared sense of purpose, bridging gaps, and creating environments where collaboration thrives. At USTRANSCOM, I noticed a recurring disconnect between IT developers and logistics personnel that was significantly slowing progress. Initially, I tried to mediate between the two groups from a distance using email and phone calls, hoping that indirect communication would resolve the issues. But it quickly became clear that this approach was not effective.

Recognizing the need for a deeper, more hands-on solution, I decided to bring the two teams closer—both figuratively and literally. The idea was simple but required stepping out of my comfort zone and leveraging my political savvy to navigate the organizational sensitivities. I facilitated embedding logistics professionals directly within the IT team to encourage real-time collaboration and direct problem-solving. This decision was not without its challenges. It required me to leverage my influencing and negotiating skills to bring together individuals with differing priorities and perspectives, and to moderate conversations that were, at times, uncomfortable but necessary to bridge the divides.

The results proved the effort worthwhile. The teams developed faster, more effective solutions through real-time interaction. More importantly, relationships between the teams grew stronger, fostering a sense of mutual respect and understanding. This experience showed me that building coalitions isn't just about breaking down silos but about creating spaces where everyone feels heard, valued, and aligned toward a common goal.

Mastering these ECQs demands more than technical skills. True success involves demonstrating the qualities and actions that represent outstanding leadership. Each challenge I encountered sharpened these skills, preparing me to create meaningful, lasting impact at the highest levels of public service.

By developing a deep understanding of each of my organizations' culture and mission, I was able to align my work with its goals while also staying updated on industry developments. It's clear to me now that building and refining skills in these five ECQs not only prepared me for leadership but also ensured my ability to create meaningful, lasting impact in an executive role.

2. CRAFT A POWERFUL RESUME

Your resume is your story distilled onto a page—a demonstration of your leadership, vision, and measurable impact. It's a showcase that proves you're the right one for the job. For me, this meant going beyond generic job descriptions and transforming my document into a narrative of achievement. For example, instead of saying I was "responsible for overseeing operations," I wrote, "streamlined team workflows, increasing efficiency by 30 percent in six months." Every detail was backed up by data, demonstrating the tangible value I brought to my roles.

To truly make your resume shine, I recommend enlisting professional support to polish your draft. SES roles demand perfection, accuracy, insight, and structure that command attention. Don't shy away from highlighting what makes you unique through special sections on significant projects or certifications. Think beyond work, too. Leadership doesn't stop at the desk. Include key volunteer roles or personal projects that illustrate your drive, vision, or creativity. And remember, every word has to serve a purpose. Make them count.

- **Example:** Instead of stating "Oversaw operations," write "Streamlined workflows, increasing efficiency by 30 percent in six months." Every detail should be backed up by data, demonstrating the tangible value you brought to your roles. For instance, when describing my contributions during Operation Desert Storm, I highlighted the impact: "Led a team that developed and delivered twenty-four critical software updates in record time, enabling seamless communication and logistics support for coalition forces."
- **Key Advice:** Highlight quantifiable achievements and unique qualifications. Use professional feedback to ensure clarity and polish. Don't shy away from highlighting what

makes you unique through special sections on significant projects or certifications. Think beyond work, too—leadership doesn't stop at the desk. Include key volunteer roles or personal projects that illustrate your drive, vision, or creativity. And remember, every word has to serve a purpose. Make them count.

3. CULTIVATE A ROBUST NETWORK

Networking doesn't come easily to everyone, and it certainly didn't come easily to me as an introvert. Imagine finding yourself at a crowded conference, eyes darting nervously around the room, yearning for invisibility. That was me. Early in my SES journey, I came to understand that building connections was not optional. Establishing strong relationships played a vital role in success.

To grow my network, I pushed myself out of comfortable spaces and into relationships that would come to define my career. I stopped sitting on the sidelines. I scheduled meetings with potential mentors, connected with colleagues to exchange ideas, and joined impactful projects where collaboration was key. If I admired someone's leadership, I reached out and learned from their expertise. By nurturing authentic connections, I built a support system that helped sharpen my skills and refine my path to the SES. This network did not rely on transactions. Mutual respect and shared growth formed the foundation of these connections.

- **Example:** At USTRANSCOM, I made a point of connecting with leaders from different military branches, learning from their diverse perspectives, and building relationships that fostered collaboration and innovation.

- **Key Advice:** Don't underestimate the power of small interactions. A casual conversation, a shared lunch, or a simple handwritten thank-you note can lay the foundation for a valuable connection.

4. EMBRACE LEADERSHIP CHALLENGES

Growing as a leader requires welcoming difficult moments and tackling them with courage. Think of leadership challenges like crucibles—tests of your resilience and problem-solving ability that mold you into something stronger. Whenever there was a tough assignment, I raised my hand, eager to step in.

A pivotal experience came when I was given the responsibility of leading a massive organizational restructure that profoundly changed team roles. The challenge was far from simple. The work was layered with obstacles, from operational complexities to team morale concerns. But these moments became defining ones. Each setback taught me patience, adaptability, and strategic foresight. With every obstacle, I grew stronger, climbed higher, and gained the kind of credibility that is essential for SES-level leadership.

- **Example:** When the WWMCCS/JOPES (Worldwide Military Command and Control System/Joint Operational Planning and Execution System) crashed during Operation Desert Storm, I immediately jumped in to lead the troubleshooting effort, even though it meant long hours and immense pressure. This experience tested my technical skills, my leadership abilities, and my resilience in the face of a critical mission failure.
- **Key Advice:** Don't shy away from challenges. Embrace them as opportunities to learn, grow, and demonstrate your leadership potential.

5. DIVERSIFY YOUR EXPERIENCE

The best leaders are those who've worn many hats and navigated different landscapes. My career was marked by deliberate steps to broaden my expertise. I've worked across technical and strategic functions, joined government and private initiatives, and embraced assignments that stretched my understanding.

Some of my most powerful lessons came from walking into new environments. Pivoting from a programmatic role in Washington to oversee production transition in St. Louis taught me agility. These moments are what transformed me into a well-rounded candidate—someone ready to face any SES challenge. No matter the discomfort, seeking out diversity of experience carves the path to becoming an exceptional leader.

- **Example:** My early work as a mathematician at the Defense Mapping Agency Aerospace Center (DMAAC) provided a solid foundation for later roles in software development and IT leadership. This diverse experience allowed me to bridge the gap between technical and strategic goals, a crucial skill for any SES candidate.
- **Key Advice:** Don't be afraid to step outside your comfort zone and explore new areas. Seek out opportunities that challenge you and broaden your perspective.

6. INVEST IN LEADERSHIP DEVELOPMENT

Learning never stops, particularly for aspiring SES members. I approached every career opportunity as a chance to expand my skills. Whether it was attending leadership courses at the Federal Executive Institute (FEI) or participating in last-minute training sessions, I refused to rest on what I already knew.

One of my guiding principles was to always say yes to

growth, even at a moment's notice. I was the first alternate for countless training opportunities, ready to step in if a seat opened up. This "Eveready" mindset helped me attend premier programs like Harvard's Senior Officials in National Security, where I gained unique perspectives on leadership at the highest levels. Those experiences fueled my leadership development, cultivating the tools and resilience I needed to thrive as an SES.

- **Example:** I was eager to take advantage of every learning opportunity. I attended every technology training session offered by Office of Personnel Management's Executive Seminar Centers, ensuring that I stayed up to date on the latest advancements in the field, expanding my knowledge base while strengthening my federal resume.
- **Key Advice:** Be proactive in seeking out learning opportunities. Attend conferences, enroll in online courses, or even shadow a leader you admire. Continuous learning is essential for growth and development.

7. PREPARE FOR INTERVIEWS

An SES interview is no ordinary meeting; it's an opportunity to demonstrate who you are and the legacy you plan to leave. To prepare, I turned my career achievements into stories—compelling, organized narratives that showcased my leadership impact. The key was to show how I did it and why it mattered.

For instance, instead of saying I "managed a team," I described how I guided a demoralized group through a turbulent transition, revitalizing performance and morale. These stories needed structure, detail, and emotional resonance. I practiced repeatedly until my delivery felt confident and natural. By the time I sat before the SES interview panel, I didn't just recite my history. I painted a vivid picture of the leader I had become and the impact I planned to make.

- **Example:** When asked about my experience with innovation, I shared the story of developing the Image Manipulation Station (IMS) at DMA, highlighting the challenges, the breakthroughs, and the ultimate impact on the agency's mission.
- **Key Advice:** Practice, practice, practice! Rehearse your stories until they flow naturally and confidently. This will help you to connect with the interview panel and showcase your leadership potential.

8. SEEK FEEDBACK

Feedback is a gift, and it was a gift I actively sought throughout my SES preparation. It was often uncomfortable for me, but I found that gaining insight from others provided clarity, uncovering weaknesses that I couldn't see. Experienced SES professionals were invaluable in this process. Their comments helped transform my ECQs and guided me through nuanced aspects of the application process.

- **Example:** One mentor pointed out that my initial resume lacked focus and didn't adequately highlight my leadership skills. Their feedback prompted me to restructure my resume, emphasizing my accomplishments and quantifying my impact with concrete metrics.
- **Key Advice:** Don't be afraid to ask for feedback, even if it's difficult to hear. Constructive criticism can help you identify blind spots and improve your candidacy.

9. BE PERSISTENT

The road to the SES isn't always smooth, and setbacks are inevitable. But every rejection taught me something valuable. I refined my application. I strengthened my interviews. Instead of viewing roadblocks as an endpoint, I embraced them as stepping stones.

Persistence requires a combination of strength and humility. Achieving success means adapting, improving, and continuing to push forward, as the future may often be found on the other side of a "no." Each attempt brought me closer to the ultimate goal while building resilience along the way.

- **Example:** When I decided to wear a tie to work, it was a small act of rebellion against the status quo. But it also sparked a shift in perception among my colleagues and superiors. Some saw it as a sign of ambition, while others viewed it with suspicion. Despite the mixed reactions, I persisted in expressing my individuality, and this ultimately led to an unexpected opportunity and a promotion.
- **Key Advice:** Don't let rejection discourage you. View it as an opportunity to learn, grow, and come back stronger. The path to the SES is often paved with perseverance.

10. LEVERAGE THE CANDIDATE DEVELOPMENT PROGRAM

The SES Candidate Development Program (CDP) wasn't a readily available option for me when I was preparing to step into an SES role, but it's a game changer for anyone considering the path today. This program offers more than just a valuable certification. The structured approach smooths the path to leadership by eliminating the challenge of OPM's after-the-fact approval of your agency's selection.

Think of it in DOD terms: As a CDP graduate, you're a "full up round," locked and loaded, ready to be deployed into the chamber of an SES leadership role. This represents more than a credential. The program serves as a strategic launchpad, positioning you as a mission-ready, vetted candidate prepared for success. If your agency offers a CDP or government-wide equivalent, take the leap. The program equips you with the skills, networks, and endorsement needed to fast-track your SES candidacy.

- **Example:** While I didn't have the opportunity to participate in a formal CDP, I sought out similar development experiences by volunteering for cross-functional teams, leading challenging projects, and seeking mentorship from senior leaders. This proactive approach helped me to build the skills and experience needed for the SES.
- **Key Advice:** If a CDP is available to you, seize the opportunity! It's a valuable investment in your future and can significantly increase your chances of success in the SES.

11. FIND A MENTOR

Behind every great leader is a mentor who guided them. I sought out SES and senior GS-15 professionals who inspired me, taking the time to learn from their careers and asking for advice. One mentor, who was also the toughest supervisor I ever had, became instrumental in refining my leadership philosophy.

Our frequent conversations turned into coaching sessions where I gained insight into leading with authenticity, navigating organizational change, and presenting myself compellingly during interviews. These relationships conveyed wisdom that no textbook could match, offering me both strategies and confidence.

- **Example:** My mentor at DMA provided technical guidance and encouraged me to think outside the box. His mentorship helped me to develop my problem-solving skills and my confidence in tackling complex challenges.
- **Key Advice:** Seek out mentors who will provide honest feedback, challenge your thinking, and support your growth. A good mentor can be a valuable asset on your journey to the SES.

12. REMAIN PATIENT

Progress toward any worthwhile goal often feels slow, and becoming an SES is no exception. I used waiting periods to my advantage, fine-tuning weaknesses and expanding my expertise. The process taught me the value of patience, not as idleness but as preparation.

This wasn't always easy for me. I'll admit, I've often struggled with impatience, especially earlier in my career. Bureaucracy, that ever-present reality of government work, was a constant test of my patience. The endless forms, the layers of approvals, the glacial pace of decision-making—these were all challenges that I, and every other civil servant, had to learn to navigate.

- **Example:** While waiting for the right opportunity to apply for an SES position, I focused on excelling in my role as a GS-15 at USTRANSCOM. I led key initiatives, mentored junior staff, and built strong relationships with mission stakeholders, demonstrating my leadership capabilities and commitment to the agency's mission.
- **Key Advice:** Don't get discouraged by setbacks or delays. Use the time to strengthen your skills, expand your network, and demonstrate your value in your current role. The right opportunity will come when you're ready.

13. STEP OUTSIDE YOUR COMFORT ZONE

Transcending comfort zones is key to growth. My willingness to take on daunting projects built my leadership resilience. I tackled uncomfortable challenges, such as leading during departmental restructuring, where tension ran high.

Every tough assignment displayed my adaptability and determination while showcasing my readiness to handle high-pressure situations with grace. The courage to lean into fear opened doors and contributed to profound personal growth.

- **Example:** When the leader of DMA's new digital cartography program visited our office, I took a leap of faith and boldly declared, "Sir, my name is Bill James. I am the best programmer in this building, and I want to work for you." This bold move, though outside my comfort zone, ultimately led to a significant career opportunity and a chance to contribute to a groundbreaking initiative.
- **Key Advice:** Don't be afraid to put yourself out there and take risks. Sometimes, the greatest rewards come from stepping outside your comfort zone and embracing the unknown.

14. MASTER THE FEDERAL BUDGET PROCESS

Success within the SES often hinges on fiscal expertise. Early on, I recognized the importance of understanding budgets. At USTRANSCOM, I designed a data-driven system that aligned workforce training expenses with mission readiness. This provided proof that strategy supported every dollar spent.

If you seek to lead at these levels, you must not only understand appropriations but also wield resources creatively to advance your agency's goals. Cultivating financial literacy through training or direct experience solidifies your ability to demonstrate high-stakes business acumen.

- **Example:** I understood that weak justifications couldn't overcome the traditional bias against funding civilian training. So, I created the Civilian Training Requirements System (CTRS), which used the command's own data to make a clear, objective case for training investments and their positive impact on mission readiness. This data-driven approach proved far more effective in securing resources and overcoming ingrained resistance.
- **Key Advice:** Take the time to learn the basics of federal budgeting. Familiarize yourself with key terms, processes, and regulations. This knowledge will not only strengthen your candidacy for the SES but also make you a more effective leader at any level.

15. CAPITALIZE ON TIMING WITH PREPAREDNESS

Timing is everything. Throughout my career, I've noticed that success often involves being in the right place at the right time. But timing isn't just about accidental luck; it's about being prepared to seize opportunities when they arise.

My career has been punctuated by moments where timing played a crucial role. For instance, my move from DMA to USTRANSCOM coincided with the establishment of the new command and its need for experienced leaders. This timing, coupled with my preparedness—my technical expertise, leadership skills, and understanding of military requirements—allowed me to step into a pivotal role and make significant contributions.

Similarly, my return to civil service at the VA aligned with the passage of the MISSION Act and the agency's urgent need for IT modernization. My private sector experience and my passion for serving veterans positioned me to lead this critical initiative and make a lasting impact.

These experiences taught me that timing can be a powerful catalyst for success, but it's only half the equation. The other half is preparedness. By continuously developing your skills, building your network, and staying informed about opportunities, you'll be ready to seize the moment when fortune smiles upon you.

- **Example:** The timing of USTRANSCOM's establishment couldn't have been better. The new command needed someone with my IT and leadership experience. This lucky break allowed me to make a significant contribution while returning to my roots in Illinois.
- **Key Advice:** Timing can be unpredictable, but you can increase your chances of encountering favorable circumstances by staying informed, networking actively, and being prepared to seize opportunities when they arise. Sometimes, the most significant turning points in your career come from recognizing and embracing the right moment. Success isn't about being lucky; it's about being ready.

FINAL THOUGHTS

The journey to the Senior Executive Service challenged me in ways I never expected. It demanded persistence, resilience, and a willingness to grow, even when the path was unclear. Each step, from mastering the ECQs to navigating setbacks and building coalitions, shaped me into the leader I aspired to be. Along the way, I learned that success does not require perfection—it comes from showing up, learning from mistakes, and staying true to your purpose. With dedication and heart, I truly believe you can too.

ABOUT THE AUTHOR

WILLIAM "BILL" JAMES's journey in public service is a testament to the extraordinary heights one can reach from the humblest beginnings. Starting as a GS-1 clerk, the lowest rung in federal service, he achieved the rare feat of climbing to the highest levels of leadership in the federal Senior Executive Service, a path very few have taken.

Over four decades, Bill served in key roles at the Defense Mapping Agency, US Transportation Command, the Pentagon, and the Department of Veterans Affairs. He modernized IT systems, pioneered digital cartography, played a critical role in supporting Operations Desert Shield and Desert Storm, and expanded healthcare access for veterans.

Bill's innovative work earned him numerous accolades, including the prestigious Fed100 award. His memoir, *The Accidental Executive*, offers inspiring lessons from his career, highlighting the profound impact of public service.

For Bill, civil service is a calling to solve critical challenges and make a tangible difference. He hopes his memoir inspires others to embrace public service and find purpose in their work.

When he's not writing, Bill enjoys exploring new technologies, genealogy, and working on vintage cars. He treasures time with his family in Vienna, Virginia, where he remains a strong advocate for public service.

www.ingramcontent.com/pod-product-compliance
Lightning Source LLC
Chambersburg PA
CBHW030442090526
44586CB00044B/546